EQUAL PAY FOR EQUAL WORK- SUPREME COURT'S LATEST LEADING CASE LAWS

CASE NOTES- FACTS- FINDINGS OF APEX COURT JUDGES & CITATIONS

JAYPRAKASH BANSILAL SOMANI

ISBN 979-888569344-8

Dedicated

To

All the Past & Present Judges of the Supreme Court of India.

Salute to their wisdom.

Salute to their interpretation of Law.

Salute to their elaborative judgement writing.

Contents

Contents

Preface

Dear Learned Advocates of the Trial Courts, Tribunals, Appellate Tribunals, High Courts, Supreme Court, HR Professionals, Corporates, Govt Recruitment Officers & Employees,

I am very delighted to provide you a book on 'Equal Pay for Equal Work-Supreme Court of India's Latest Leading Case Laws'.

In this book you will get...

1. Name of the Case i. e. Cause title

2.Relevant Sections discussed in the case

3.Hon'ble Judges/Coram of the case

4.Number of PDF Pages in Original Judgement of the case

5. All available Citations of the case

6. Case Note with appeal allowed/ dismissed or disposed off

7. Facts of the case

8.Hon'ble Apex Court's findings, while dismissing/allowing or disposing the appeal

9. Ratio Decidendi if any.

My special thanks to Manupatra, because of their web portal I can compile this book in well manner. I am also thankful to Notion Press to support me to publish & market this book throughout the Country. Thanks to my Juniors, Advocate Colleagues & Insolvency Professional Colleagues to support me in this venture.

Miss Devpriya Shah has helped me a lot to compile this book.

I hope this book will add some value addition in the wealth of your legal knowledge. Your positive feedbacks will boost me to compile/ write further books & negative feedbacks will improve my skills. Kindly send your valuable feedbacks by email.

Thanks with Regards,

Jayprakash B. Somani

Advocate, Supreme Court of India

Email: jaysomani64@gmail.com

Web Site:www.jayprakashsomani.com

Call: 8384051134, 9322188701, 9318381287

Acknowledgements

Printed & Published by
Notion Press
No. 8, 3rd Cross Street,
CIT Colony, Mylapore,
Chennai, Tamil Nadu- 600004

ÞÞÞ

Managed by
Jayprakash Somani Advocates & Solicitors
Law Firm for Supreme Court of India
Delhi Office
257 C, Pocket 1, Mayur Vihar Phase 1, Delhi 110091.
Call 8384051134, 9322188701, 8459194576, 01141051516
Supreme Court Chamber
312, 3rd Floor, M. C. Setalvad Block, In front of 'D' Gate, Bhagwan Das Road, Supreme Court of India, New Delhi 110001
Contact: 8459194576, 9811011747
www.jayprakashsomani.com

ÞÞÞ

Books are available online at
1. **Notion Press:** https://notionpress.com/author/jayprakash_somani
2. **Amazon:** https://www.amazon.in/s?k=jayprakash+somani
3. **Flipkart:** https://www.flipkart.com/search?q=Jayprakash%20Somani

ÞÞÞ

ONE

Punjab State Co-operative Milk Producers Federation Ltd. and Ors. Vs. Balbir Kumar Walia and Ors., 2021

Hon'ble Judges/Coram:

Sanjay Kishan Kaul and Hemant Gupta, JJ.

Equivalent Citation: AIR2021SC3316, 2021(4)ALT230, 2021(4)BLJ328, 2021(III)CLR1, 2021(3)ESC670(SC), 2021(3)J.L.J.R.250, 2021LabIC3046, 2021(3)PLJR202, (2021)8SCC784, 2021(3)SCT322(SC), 2021(2)SLJ427(SC), 2021(5)SLR881(SC), MANU/SC/0413/2021

Relevant sections: Article 12 of the Constitution of India; Punjab State Co-operative Milk Producers Federation Services (Common Cadre) Rules, 1980[3]

Number of pages in original Judgment: 20

Case Note:

Service - Administrative Decision - Scope of Judicial Review - Payment as per Revised Pay Scale - Federation Appellant directed to grant Respondent employees benefits of revised pay scale - Federation cited difficulty due to financial stress during the relevant period - High Court directed Federation to pay revised pay scale since period claimed by employees - Plea of financial stress declined - Hence, the present appeal - Whether High Court in exercise of power to judicial review can interfere into administrative realm of state?

Brief Facts:

The present appeals were filed against the impugned order allowing writ petitions of Respondent-Employees holding that the Punjab State Co-operative Milk Producers Federation Ltd. (Federation)/ Appellant is a State within the meaning of Article 12 of the Constitution of India. Employees were therefore held to be entitled to pay scale equivalent to their counterparts in the State of Punjab from1.1.1986, though the revised pay scale was allowed by the Federation w.e.f. 1.1.1994.The main grievance of the Federation was regarding grant of revised pay scale w.e.f. 1.1.1986 as Federation was suffering with acute financial stringency in those days and had therefore granted revised pay scales from 1.1.1994.High Court allowed the writ petitions filed by employees holding that the financial stringency was no longer an excuse to not revise the pay scales and thus held that the date of implementation to grant revised pay scales as 1.1.1994 was absolutely unfair. The Federation has filed the present appeal against such order.

Held, while allowing the Appeals:

i. CIVIL APPEAL No. 7427, 7429, 7430, 7431, 7433AND 7435 OF 2011 The decision that Federation was in financial difficulties is based upon relevant material before the Federation. The process to arrive at such decision can be said to be flawed only on the permissible grounds of illegality, irrationality and procedural impropriety. Neither the decision-making process, nor the decision itself suffers from any such vice.
ii. The income generated by the Federation is not to be expanded only on payment of salary but is also required for upgradation of technology, renovation and expansion of plants etc. Therefore, entire profit is not to be appropriated towards the wages of the employees alone. The Federation was established as a step towards white revolution. The employees are facilitators of the employer to achieve such objective and thus demanding enhanced wages without considering the objective and financial condition of the employer would not be ideal.
iii. High Court granted revised pay scales with effect from 01.01.1986 instead of revised pay scales granted to the employees of the federation with

effect from 01.01.1994. Therefore, restricting it for a period of 3 years and 2 months will not be helpful in respect of the financial condition of the Federation as during the relevant time the federation was suffering from huge losses.

iv. In view of the above, order of the High Court unjustified and in excess of the power of judicial review conferred on the High Court. Consequently, the appeals are allowed.

v. CIVIL APPEAL No. 7432 OF 2011 Educational qualifications and the responsibilities of the two posts are quite different. Therefore, the principle of equal pay for equal work would not be applicable to them inasmuch as Grade I is a higher post having higher duties and responsibilities than Grade II.

vi. No merit in the argument claiming equal pay for the alleged equal work. Consequently, the appeal is allowed.

vii. CIVIL APPEAL No. 7434 OF 2011 Order passed by the High Court has not been challenged in appeal by the employees. Secondly, the classification of different pay scales is permissible based upon educational qualifications, experience and nature of duties. In view of the said facts, employees not entitled to the pay scale as claimed in the writ petition. Appeal allowed. The orders passed by the High Court set aside.

PPP

TWO

UNION OF INDIA (UOI) AND ORS. VS. MANOJ KUMAR AND ORS., 2021

Hon'ble Judges/Coram:

Sanjay Kishan Kaul and Hrishikesh Roy, JJ.

Equivalent Citation: 2021(3)J.L.J.R.395, 2021(3)J.L.J.R.395, (2021)7MLJ4, 2021(3)PLJR387, 2021(4)SCT53(SC), MANU/SC/0583/2021

Relevant sections: Rule 107 of the Indian Railway Establishment Code

Number of pages in original Judgment: 08

Case Note:

Service - Pay parity - Disparity between Secretariat and Field offices - Recommendations of Sixth Central Pay Commission (6th CPC) - Whether claims raised by Appellant considering pay parity sustainable?

Brief Facts:

The present matter came up in reference to claims made by Private Secretaries (Grade-II) (PS-II) employed in the Eastern Central Railways (Field Office/ Zonal Railways) , for parity in pay with their counterparts working in the Central Secretariat Stenographers Service ("CSSS")/ Railway Board Secretariat Stenographers Service ("RBSSS")/ Central Administrative Tribunal ("CAT"). Claim referred 6th CPC as the base to seek parity.

Held, while allowing the Appeal:

i. The Pay Commission is a specialized body set up with the objective of resolving anomalies. It is relevant to note that the anomaly in question was referred to the Pay Commission at the request of candidates similarly situated to the Respondents and thus, the 6th CPC was aware of the claim for parity and the requirement of making a recommendation in that regard. In its wisdom while giving better scales it has still sought to maintain a separate recommendation for non-Secretariat Organizations.

ii. Aspect of disparity between the Secretariat and the field offices was a matter taken note of by the Commission itself while making the recommendations. Yet to some extent, a separate recommendation was made qua Secretariat Organizations and non-Secretariat Organizations. Once these recommendations are separately made, to direct absolute parity would be to make the separate recommendations qua non-Secretariat Organizations otiose. If one may say, there would have been no requirement to make these separate recommendations if everyone was to be treated on parity on every aspect.

iii. Impugned judgment unsustainable and accordingly set aside. Appeals allowed.

PPP

THREE

UNION OF INDIA (UOI) AND ORS. VS. BALBIR SINGH, 2020

Hon'ble Judges/Coram:

L. Nageswara Rao and Hemant Gupta, JJ.

Equivalent Citation: AIR2020SC469, 2020(2)BLJ61, 2020(1)ESC88(SC), [2020(166)FLR925], 2020(1)SCT721(SC), 2020(1)SLJ400(SC), 2020(4)SLR201(SC), MANU/SC/0040/2020

Relevant sections: Rule 3 of the IDSE Rules

Number of pages in original Judgment: 04

Case Note:

Service - Direction - Legality - Rule 3 of the IDSE Rules - Present appeal was directed against judgment of Armed Forces Tribunal, by which Appellants were directed to consider claim of Respondent for payment of grade pay of Rs. 10,000 or more, at par with his civilian counterparts holding post of Chief Engineer in the Military Engineering Services (MES), with all consequential benefits - Whether impugned direction was liable to be set aside.

Brief Facts:

The Respondent was commissioned in the Army on 16.12.1978 and he was allotted to the Corps of Engineers in July, 2005. The Respondent was promoted to the rank of Brigadier and was posted as Chief Engineer, Shillong Zone in the Military Engineering Service. Aggrieved by the disparity with regard to grade pay of Brigadier vis-a-vis civilian Chief Engineer in the MES, the Respondent filed O.A. before the Armed Forces

Tribunal, Regional Bench, Jaipur and sought a direction to the Appellants that he shall be entitled to the grade pay of Rs. 10,000 at par with his civilian counterparts. The Respondent further sought a direction to the Appellants herein to pay the arrears consequent to re-fixation of grade pay at Rs. 10,000 with all benefits along with interest at 18% on such arrears. The O.A. filed before the Armed Forces Tribunal, Regional Bench, Jaipur was transferred to the Armed Forces Tribunal, Regional Bench, Kolkata. By a judgment, the Tribunal allowed the O.A. filed by the Respondent and granted the relief sought by the Respondent. The application filed by the Appellants seeking leave to appeal to this Court was dismissed by the Tribunal. Learned Additional Solicitor General appearing for the Appellants-Union of India argued that an Army Officer posted as Chief Engineer in the MES cannot seek parity of grade pay with his civilian counterparts in the Indian Defence Service of Engineers (IDSE) because members of the Armed Forces are a distinct and distinguishable class.

Held, while allowing the appeal:

i. The IDSE Rules regulate the method of recruitment and conditions of service of persons appointed to the Indian Defence Service of Engineers in the Ministry of Defence, Government of India. Rule 3 of the IDSE Rules deals with the constitution of the Indian Defence Service of Engineers. The service in the Indian Defence Service of Engineers, according to Rule 3, shall consist of posts specified in Schedule I. The post of Chief Engineer, Senior Administrative Grade is shown against Serial No. 3 of Schedule-I. The total number of posts of Chief Engineers are 45. The pay scale of Chief Engineer, Senior Administrative Grade is Rs. 37400-67000 in pay band - 4. The grade pay applicable to the post of Chief Engineer, Senior Administrative Grade is Rs. 10,000. It is categorically laid down in Rule 12 of the IDSE Rules that the Rules shall not apply to Army Officers appointed on a tenure basis as they are governed by the Army Act and the Rules framed thereunder. There is no dispute that the Respondent was appointed on a tenure basis in accordance with the MES Regulations. Therefore, there cannot be any doubt that the IDSE Rules are not applicable to the Respondent. As such, we are unable to accept the submission made on behalf of the Respondent that the IDSE Rules are applicable only to the 15 civilian posts and not to the others.

ii. The Army Officers forming a separate class in comparison to the civilian employees is a point which is no more res integra. In Confederation of

Ex. Servicemen Associations (supra) and Union of India v. Capt. Gurdev Singh, this Court has clearly laid down that the classification of military personnel as different class from non-military personnel is permissible and valid. The submissions made on behalf of the Appellant that the Army Officers serving in the MES as Chief Engineers continue to get the same benefits and perks attached to the post of Brigadier has not been controverted by the Respondent. Though there is no dispute that the principle of 'equal pay for equal work' is applicable even to tenure or temporary appointments, in view of the IDSE Rules which govern the grade pay of the post of the Chief Engineer, Senior Administrative Grade, we are of the opinion that the Respondent is not entitled to claim parity with members of the IDSE. The validity of the IDSE Rules has not been challenged by the Respondent. Present Court do not see any force in the submission of the Respondent that grade pay should be made available to all persons working as Chief Engineers irrespective of the source. Respondent continues to be a Brigadier for all practical purposes and is entitled for the benefits attached to the post of Brigadier, irrespective of the place and post in which he works.

iii. The judgment of the Armed Forces Tribunal is set aside and the appeal is allowed.

ÞÞÞ

FOUR

UNION OF INDIA (UOI) AND ORS.VS. M.V. MOHANAN NAIR, 2020

Hon'ble Judges/Coram:

R. Banumathi, A.S. Bopanna and Hrishikesh Roy, JJ.

Equivalent Citation: 2020(6)ABR751, AIR2020SC5107, 2020(2)ALT144, 2021LabIC3347, (2020)5SCC421, (2020)2SCC(LS)1, 2020 (4) SCJ 10, 2020(2)SCT366(SC), 2020(2)SLJ217(SC), 2020(5)SLR755(SC), MANU/SC/0281/2020

Relevant sections: Rule 3(7) of Central Civil Services (Revised Pay) Rules, 2008

Number of pages in original Judgment: 17

Case Note:

Service - Financial upgradation - Promotional post - High Courts dismissing petitions filed by Appellants, thereby upholding decisions rendered by different Benches of Tribunal granting financial upgradation of grade pay in next promotional hierarchy by placing reliance upon Union of India and Ors. v. Raj Pal and Anr. - Hence, present appeal - Whether Modified Assured Career Progression (MACP) Scheme entitles financial upgradation to next grade pay or to grade pay of next promotional hierarchy.

Brief Facts:

The High Courts dismissing petitions filed by the Appellants, thereby upholding decisions rendered by different Benches of Central Administrative Tribunal granting financial upgradation of grade pay in the next promotional hierarchy by placing reliance upon Union of India and

Ors. v. Raj Pal and Anr. All the Tribunals/High Courts had only relied upon Raj Pal's case for grant of financial upgradation on promotional hierarchy and rejected the stand of the Appellant that under MACP scheme, the employees were entitled to financial upgradation of the next grade pay only.

Held, while allowing the appeals:

i. The change in policy brought about by supersession of ACP Scheme with the MACP Scheme was after consideration of all the disparities and the representations of the employees. The Sixth Central Pay Commission was an expert body which has comprehensively examined all the issues and the representations as also the issue of stagnation and at the same time to promote efficiency in the functioning of the departments. MACP Scheme had been introduced on the recommendation of the Sixth Central Pay Commission which had been accepted by the Government of India. After accepting the recommendation of the Sixth Central Pay Commission, the ACP Scheme was withdrawn and the same was superseded by the MACP Scheme. This was not some random exercise which is unilaterally done by the Government, rather, it was based on the opinion of the expert body - Sixth Central Pay Commission which had examined all the issues, various representations and disparities. Before making the recommendation for the Pay Scale/Revised Pay Scale, the Pay Commission takes into consideration the existing pay structure, the representations of the government servants and various other factors after which the recommendations were made. When the expert body like Pay Commission had comprehensively examined all the issues and representations and also took note of inter-departmental disparities owing to varying promotional hierarchies, the court should not interfere with the recommendations of the expert body. When the government had accepted the recommendation of the Pay Commission and had also implemented those, any interference by the court would have a serious impact on the public exchequer.

The ACP Scheme which was now superseded by MACP Scheme was a matter of government policy. Interference with the recommendations of the expert body like Pay Commission and its recommendations for the MACP, would have serious impact on the public exchequer. The recommendations of the Pay Commission for MACP Scheme had been accepted by the

Government and implemented. There was nothing to show that the Scheme was arbitrary or unjust warranting interference. Without considering the advantages in the MACP Scheme, the High Courts erred in interfering with the government's policy in accepting the recommendations of the Sixth Central Pay Commission by simply placing reliance upon Raj Pal's case. The impugned orders could not be sustained and were liable to be set aside.

ᕈᕈᕈ

FIVE

Chief Regional Manager, United India Insurance Company Limited Vs. Siraj Uddin Khan, 2019

Hon'ble Judges/Coram:

Ashok Bhushan and Navin Sinha, JJ.

Equivalent Citation: AIR2019SC3388, 2019(6) ALJ 675, 2019(4)ALT285, 2019 5 AWC4134SC, 2019(III)CLR358, 2019(3)ESC707(SC), [2020(164)FLR64], 2019LabIC3210, 2019(9)SCALE273, (2019)7SCC564, (2019)2SCC(LS)431, 2019 (8) SCJ 335, 2019(3)SCT542(SC), 2019(5)SLR216(SC), (2019)4WBLR(SC)188, MANU/SC/0899/2019

Relevant sections: Rule 23(a) of the General Insurance (Conduct, Discipline & Appeal) Rules, 1975;

Number of pages in original Judgment: 09

Case Note:

Service - Arrears of salary - Direction to pay - Present appeal had been filed challenging judgment of High Court, partly allowing writ petition of Respondent, wherein direction had been issued by High Court for payment of arrears of salary and other benefits -Whether High Court committed error in directing for payment of salary after 14th May, 2009 to 20th June, 2012

Brief Facts:

Challenge in present case is relating to entitlement for payment of salary after 14th May, 2009 to 20th June, 2012. Appellant submits that, High Court committed error in directing for payment of salary after 14th May, 2009 to 20th June, 2012, whereas the Respondent absented from work during the period and was clearly not entitled for payment of salary on the principle of "No Work No Pay". Present is not a case where by virtue of any order terminating the services of the Respondent, he could not work. With regard to salary after 14th May, 2009 till 20th June, 2012, learned Single Judge has not adjudicated the claim except observing that in view of the judgment of High Court dated 29th May, 2015 against which special leave petition was dismissed, Respondent was entitled for arrears of salary. He further submits that, the fact that by virtue of the judgment of learned Single Judge dated 29th May, 2015, Respondent has to be treated in service does not automatically result in any direction to pay the salary, since no such direction was issued in the judgment of learned Single Judge dated 29th May, 2015. The payment of salary for the aforesaid period does not automatically flow from the judgment of learned Single Judge.

Held, while allowing the appeal in part:

i. There is no adjudication regarding claim of salary or back wages to the Respondent in the impugned judgment of learned Single Judge for the period 15th May, 2009 to 20th June, 2012. Learned Single Judge was of the opinion that in view of the setting aside of the order dated 26.06.2012, payment of salary is automatic, which view of the Single Judge is not correct. The present is not a case where the Respondent was dismissed from the service and consequent to dismissal, he could not work and when dismissal was set aside, he will be automatically entitled for back wages.
ii. Present is not a case where Respondent was kept away from the work on account of dismissal. Admittedly, the Respondent attained the age of retirement on 20.06.2012 and order terminating his services was passed only on 26.06.2012, which was rightly held to be ineffective.
iii. In the present case, Respondent was not kept away from work by any order of the Appellant. The order of termination of his services/dismissal was passed on 26.06.2012, after his retirement on 20.06.2012, which in no manner prohibited the Respondent from working. The Respondent

during submission has submitted that he was illegally transferred to Branch Office, Jaunpur from Allahabad. He was suffering from a disability of more than 40% and he could not have been transferred to another place. There is nothing on record to indicate that transfer of Respondent from Branch Office, Allahabad to Branch Office, Jaunpur was at any time set aside or withdrawn. The salary upto 14th May, 2009 was allowed to the Respondent on account of setting aside of the order dated 14th May, 2009, which was with all consequential benefits but with regard to entitlement of salary after 14th May, 2009 to 20th June, 2012, there has been no adjudication by the High Court, which is apparent from judgment of the High Court dated 03.07.2018.

Learned Single Judge having itself not determined the entitlement of Respondent to receive salary after 14th May, 2009 to 20th June, 2012, it ought to have directed the Appellant to consider the entitlement and take a decision thereon. Ends of justice be served in setting aside the direction of the High Court directing the Appellant to make payment of salary after 14th May, 2009 to 20th June, 2012, with a direction to the Appellant to consider the claim of Respondent for back wages after 14th May, 2009 to 20th June, 2012 and pass appropriate orders giving reasons within three months. The appeal is partly allowed.

PPP

SIX

Punjab State Power Corporation Limited Vs. Rajesh Kumar Jindal and Ors., 2019

Hon'ble Judges/Coram:

R. Banumathi and Indira Banerjee, JJ.

Equivalent Citation: 2019(1)ESC65(SC), 2019(1)SCALE218, (2019)3SCC547, (2019)1SCC(LS)503, 2019 (3) SCJ 562, 2019(1)SCT536(SC), 2019(1)SLJ149(SC), 2019(2)SLR410(SC), 2019 (1) WLN 68 (SC), MANU/SC/0028/2019

Relevant sections: Article 14 of Constitution of India; Regulation 3(g) of Punjab State Electricity Board (Revised Pay) Regulations, 1988

Number of pages in original Judgment: 13

Case Note:

Service - Pay-scale - Revision thereof - Present appeals arose out of judgment passed by High Court dismissing appeals and order in review petition dismissing review filed by Appellant-Board by holding that, Special Leave Petition involving same issue i.e. parity of pay scale was already pending before Supreme Court - Whether Internal Auditors were entitled to claim parity of pay scale with Head Clerks and Head Clerk-cum-Divisional Accountants irrespective of nature of recruitment, qualifications and nature of duties and responsibilities - Could Internal Auditors claim equity of pay scale, merely because they were in same group (Class-XII) irrespective of nature of work and internal qualification for recruitment.

Brief Facts:

Parity in pay scales of two posts - Head Clerks and Internal Auditors in Group XII of Punjab State Electricity Board (PSEB) was subject matter of issue in present appeals. Aggrieved by order issued by Appellant-Board and alleging disparity and violation of Article 14 of Constitution of India, Respondents preferred Civil Writ Petition before High Court, contending that Internal Auditors, Head Clerks as well as Sub Fire Officers belong to same group viz. Group XII and that Internal Auditors were always on par with Head Clerks being promotional post from post of Circle Assistants/ ARAs Group XII. Learned Single Judge vide judgment allowed filed by Sub Fire Officers by holding that till some point of time, persons working as Head Clerks, Head Clerk-cum-Divisional Accountants and Internal Auditors were given same scale of pay and therefore, parity of scale of pay could not be denied to Sub Fire Officers when scales were increased for other three classes of persons within Group XII. Against order, Appellant-Board preferred LPA which came to be dismissed. Aggrieved by judgment, Appellant preferred SLP(C) before this Court wherein, notice was issued and same was pending for consideration before this Court. Learned Single Judge of High Court by its order allowed Civil Writ Petition filed by Respondents-Internal Auditors claiming parity of pay scale with Head Clerks on erroneous assumption that Respondents were Sub Fire Officers or similarly situated as Sub Fire Officers who were seeking parity of wages with other persons. In present appeals, question involved was parity of pay scale between Head Clerks and Internal Auditors.

Held, while allowing the appeal:

i. Ordinarily, courts will not enter upon task of job evaluation which was generally left to expert bodies like Pay Commission etc. aggrieved employees claiming parity must establish thaty were unjustly treated by arbitrary action or discriminated.
ii. Burden of proof in establishing parity in pay scales and nature of duties and responsibilities was on person claiming such right. Person claiming parity must produce material before court to prove that nature of duties and functions were similar and that, they were entitled to parity of pay scales. It was duty of an employee seeking parity of pay to prove and establish that he had been discriminated against.

iii. The duties and nature of work of Head Clerks and Internal Auditors were entirely different. Head Clerk works under XEN, Drawing and Disbursement Officer and there was only one Head Clerk in Division Office. Head Clerk was Head of establishment in Divisional Office and total work of establishment was under control of Head Clerk. Head Clerk disbursed salaries and other payments of Sub-divisions and Division Offices and also maintains leave and other miscellaneous works for Sub-divisions and Division Offices and discharges administrative functions and thus, had more responsibilities. Per contra, Internal Auditor works under control of Chief Auditor. Duty of Internal Auditor was to audit billing of Revenue Department of Sub-division Office which included billing of domestic supply to large supply. Internal Auditors work in Sub-division and there could be one or more Internal Auditors as per quantity of work.

iv. It was duty of an employee seeking parity of scale of pay to prove that educational qualifications required for both posts, mode of recruitment and nature of work performed by them were one and same.re were neither pleadings nor any material produced by Respondents to prove that nature of work performed by Internal Auditors was similar with that of Head Clerks. In writ petition, Respondents had claimed parity of pay scale only on ground that, they were categorised in Group XII along with Head Clerks. Merely on ground that cadre of Internal Auditors were placed in Group XII along with Head Clerks, could not be a ground for seeking parity of pay scale.

v. Equation of posts and revision of pay scale was within domain of Government. Matter should be left to discretion and expertise of Pay Committee and Government to take decision on scale of pay/revision of pay scale by considering nature of duties and responsibilities. As pointed out earlier, Pay Anomaly Committee had given elaborate reasons for revising pay scales of Head Clerks and Internal Auditors. Conclusion arrived at by experts/Pay Anomaly Committee were not susceptible to judicial review and courts were not to interfere with decision of Government which was based on opinion of experts.

vi. Exercise of option for promotion as Internal Auditor was a "conscious option". Further, it was always open to Appellant-Board to revise scale of pay in terms of Regulation 3(g) of Punjab State Electricity Board (Revised Pay) Regulations, 1988.

vii. Learned Single Judge proceeded under erroneous footing as if case of Internal Auditors was covered by case put forth by Sub Fire Officers. Learned Single Judge did not keep in view counter statement filed by Appellant-Board before High Court pointing out various distinguishing features of Internal Auditors and Head Clerks on account of which no parity could be granted to Internal Auditors with Head Clerks. High Court also did not keep in view that Pay Anomaly Committee did consider demand of Internal Auditors and had not accepted demand in view of different nature of duties and various other relevant factors. learned Single Judge erred in recording that Respondents were in same category of "Sub Fire Officers" within same group which had been decided by earlier judgment.

viii. Merely because various different posts had been categorized under Group XII, they could not claim parity of pay scale as that of Head Clerk. All more so, when Internal Auditors were appointed 55% by direct recruitment and 45% by promotion from Circle Assistant/Assistant Revenue Accountant. High Court did not keep in view that duties, nature of work and promotion channel of Head Clerks and Internal Auditors were entirely different and that option to seek promotion apparently as Internal Auditors was "conscious exercise of option", impugned judgment cannot be sustained and was liable to be set aside.

ix. Impugned judgment passed by High Court and Order in review petition were set aside. Appeals allowed.

PPP

SEVEN

Punjab State Electricity Board and Ors. Vs. Thana Singh and Ors., 2019

Hon'ble Judges/Coram:

R. Banumathi and Indira Banerjee, JJ.

Equivalent Citation: AIR2019SC354, 2019(2)ALLMR474, 2019(1)ESC58(SC), 2019(1)J.L.J.R.297, 2019LabIC782, 2019(5)MhLj1, 2019(3)MPLJ519, 2019(2)PLJR2, 2019(1)SCALE244, (2019)4SCC113, (2019)1SCC(LS)582, 2019 (5) SCJ 103, 2019(1)SCT517(SC), 2019(1)SLJ55(SC), 2019(2)SLR327(SC), 2019(1)UC3, MANU/SC/0029/2019

Relevant sections: Article 14 of Constitution of India

Number of pages in original Judgment: 09

Case Note:

Service - Pay-scale - Revision thereof - Present appeal arose out of judgment passed by High Court dismissing LPA on ground that, Respondents-Sub Fire Officers were entitled to parity of scales of pay as pay scale granted/revised to other classes of posts within same group viz., Group XII of Punjab State Electricity Board - Whether Sub Fire Officers could claim parity of pay scale with pay scale of Head Clerks, Head Clerk-cum-Divisional Accountants, Internal Auditors, etc. merely on ground that post of Sub Fire Officers was categorised in Group XII -Whether Respondents were right in contending that, grant of different scale of pay to Sub Fire Officers was discrimination and in violation of Article 14 of Constitution of India. Facts: Respondents-Sub Fire Officers submitted various representations to Appellant-Board requesting for higher pay scale on ground that pay scale to post of Sub Fire Officers in Punjab State Government Department i.e. Fire Protection Department was Rs. 1800-3200 and therefore, Respondents-Sub Fire Officers working in Appellant-Board were also to be given same scale of pay. Respondents-Sub Fire Officers filed petition stating that action of Appellant-Board in granting pay scale less than State Government employees was illegal, unjustified, discriminatory and violative of Article 14 of Constitution of India. Learned Single Judge allowed writ petition holding that Sub Fire Officers were within Group XII that included Head Clerks, Head Clerk-cum-Divisional Accountants, Internal Auditors, etc. therefore, Sub Fire Officers could not be denied same scales of pay when increased for other three classes of persons within Group XII. However, learned Single Judge rejected Respondent's plea claiming parity with employees of State Government. Observing that Respondents were to be treated on par with other three classes within Group XII of Board, learned Single Judge allowed writ petition. Division Bench of High Court dismissed appeal filed by Appellant-Board holding that, there was no basis for differently treating Sub Fire Officers included in Group XII.

Held, while allowing the appeal:

i. It was fairly well settled that equation of pay scales must be left to Government and on decision of experts and Court should not interfere with it. Observing that equation of pay scales of posts must be left to Government and experts, in.
ii. In light of above principles, case of Sub Fire Officers in PSEB required to be examined whether they were entitled to parity in pay scales as that of Head Clerks, Head Clerk-cum-Divisional Accountants, Internal Auditors, etc. PSEB was an autonomous body constituted by Notification of Punjab Government under Section 5 of Electricity Supply Act, 1948 and services under PSEB were governed by Punjab State Electricity Board (Revised Pay) Regulations, 1988. First Schedule relates to categorisation of various groups and revised scales of pay for categories specified thereunder.
iii. In year 1988, though post of Sub Fire Officers had been included in Group XII in one category as that of Head Clerks, Head Clerk-cum-Divisional Accountants and Internal Auditors, nature of work, duties, responsibilities and initial qualifications for recruitment and manner

of recruitment to each post were different since all these posts belong to different cadre. Respondents cannot claim as a matter of right that, they should be given similar pay scale as were given to categories of posts such as Head Clerks, Head Clerk-cum-Divisional Accountants and Internal Auditors.

iv. Duties and nature of work of Head Clerks and Internal Auditors were entirely different. Head Clerk works under XEN, Drawing and Disbursement Officer and there was only one Head Clerk in Division Office. Head Clerk was Head of establishment in Divisional Office and total work of establishment was under control of Head Clerk. Head Clerk also maintains leave and other miscellaneous works for Sub-divisions and Division Offices and also discharges administrative functions and thus, had more responsibilities. Duty of an Internal Auditor was to audit billing of Revenue Department of Sub-division Office which includes billing of domestic supply to large supply. Whereas duty of Sub Fire Officer was entirely different viz., rush to spot of emergency along with fire-fighting equipment crew, direct and supervise fire-fighting and rescue operations, arrange for extra fire fighting equipments, if need be discharge mechanical foam, dry chemical powder, etc. and inform fire pump house for continuous running of pumps and also inform Fire Officer/Sr.Xen/Fire and Safety regarding incident. Thus, work performed by Sub Fire Officer was entirely different from nature of duties performed by Head Clerks and Internal Auditors.

v. Appellant-Board being an autonomous body governed by its own Regulations, it was for Board to classify its employees/posts on basis of qualifications, duties and responsibilities of posts concerned. If classification had reasonable nexus with objective sought to be achieved, Board would be justified in prescribing different pay scales. Article 14 of Constitution of India would be applicable only when discrimination was made out between persons who were similarly situated and not otherwise. It was duty of an employee seeking parity of pay to prove and establish that, they had been discriminated.

vi. Person claiming parity must produce material before court to prove that nature of duties and functions were similar and that, they were entitled to parity of pay scales.

vii. Burden of establishing parity in pay scale and employment was on person claiming such right.re were neither pleadings nor any material produced by Respondents to prove that nature of work performed by Sub

Fire Officers was similar with that of Head Clerks and Internal Auditors to claim parity of pay scale. Burden lies upon party who claims parity of pay scale to prove similarity in duties and responsibilities. In writ petition, Respondents had only claimed parity of pay scale with those of employees working under Punjab Government which was not accepted by learned Single Judge. Determination of parity or disparity in duties and responsibilities was a complex issue and same should be left to expert body. When expert body considered revision of pay for various posts, it did not revise pay scale of Sub Fire Officers. When expert body had taken such a view, it was not for courts to substitute its views and interfere with same and take a different view.

viii. Though Head Clerks, Head Clerk-cum-Divisional Accountants and Internal Auditors were earlier placed in same group viz. Group XII; but educational qualifications requisite for these posts and mode of recruitment were different. Likewise, there was no similarity in work performed by employees on those posts. Only in cases of complete similarity in nature of work, duties, responsibilities and promotional channels, parity of pay scale can be claimed. Merely on ground that Sub Fire Officers were categorised in Group XII along with Head Clerks, Head Clerk-cum-Divisional Accountants and Internal Auditors could not be a ground for seeking parity of pay scale. As submitted by learned Senior Counsel for Appellant-Board, nature of work, duties, responsibilities and initial qualification for recruitment of each post were entirely different as all these posts belong to different cadre.

ix. Though in year 1988, there were only four posts in Group XII, number of several posts had been subsequently included. For all these posts, source and mode of recruitment, qualifications and nature of work were entirely different. High Court, erred in not keeping in view financial consequences of direction to give parity of pay scale to Sub Fire Officers.

x. In writ petition, Respondents had taken plea that, they were entitled to scale of pay on par with employees of Punjab Government in parity of wages. Nature of work performed by those in service of Punjab Government were different from those in service of Board, learned Single Judge rightly refused to accept plea of Respondents claiming parity with employees of State Government.

xi. Learned Single Judge, however, proceeded under erroneous footing that merely because Sub Fire Officers were categorised in Group XII, they were entitled parity of scale of pay with pay scale of Head Clerks, Head

Clerk-cum-Divisional Accountants and Internal Auditors. Inclusion of posts of Sub Fire Officers in Group XII may not be a determinative factor to hold that Sub Fire Officers were equal with Head Clerks, Head Clerk-cum-Divisional Accountants, and Internal Auditors. Mere difference in pay scale does not always amount to discrimination; it depends upon mode of selection/recruitment, nature, quality of work and duties and that status of both posts were identical.

xii. Respondents had not produced any material to show that, there was any similarity/identity between posts of Sub Fire Officers and Head Clerks, Head Clerk-cum-Divisional Accountants and Internal Auditors in terms of nature of duties, responsibilities, qualifications and mode of recruitment etc. to apply principle of parity of pay scale. Learned Single Judge did not keep in view that nature of duties and responsibilities performed by Sub Fire Officers were different and parity cannot be claimed merely on ground that, they were categorised in one group. Judgment of learned Single Judge and impugned judgment of Division Bench could not be sustained and were liable to be set aside.

xiii. Impugned judgment passed by High Court was set aside. Appeal allowed.

ÞÞÞ

EIGHT

BADRI VISHAL PANDEY AND ORS. VS. RAJESH MITTAL AND ORS., 2019

Hon'ble Judges/Coram:

A.M. Khanwilkar and Hemant Gupta, JJ.

Equivalent Citation: AIR2019SC289, 2019(2) ALJ 316, 2019(I)CLR723, [2019(160)FLR645], 2019(1)SCALE155, (2019)16SCC360, 2019(1)SCT550(SC), (2019)1UPLBEC1, MANU/SC/0010/2019

Relevant sections: Section 6N of the U.P. Industrial Disputes Act, 1947

Number of pages in original Judgment: 07

Case Note:

Contempt of Court - Termination - Disobedience of order - Petitioners were engaged as daily wager in U.P. Jal Nigam facing retrenchment of their services in pursuance to decision taken by Board - In pursuance to decision taken by Board Petitioner's services had been terminated - Writ petition was filed before High Court challenging order of termination which stand dismissed - Petitioner No. 1 raised industrial dispute which was referred to Labour Court - Labour Court ordered to pay compensation - Such Award was challenged by filing Writ Petition before High Court - In writ petition, order was of reinstatement but without back-wages - Jal Nigam filed Special Leave Petition against order of Single Bench - Such Special Leave Petitions were decided on basis of office order wherein it was resolved that in future, as and when any vacancy arises on daily wages/muster roll, preference would be given to terminated/retrenched employee of department - Hence, present contempt petition - Whether Respondents had violated any order passed by this Court.

Brief Facts:

The Petitioners were engaged as daily wager in the U.P. Jal Nigam sometime in the year 1989 on various dates facing retrenchment of their services in pursuance to decision taken by the Board. U.P. Jal Nigam. Accordingly, in pursuance to decision taken by the Board Petitioner's services had been terminated. A Writ petition was filed before the High Court challenging order of termination which stand dismissed. The Petitioner No. 1 raised an industrial dispute which was referred to Labour Court. The Labour Court ordered to pay compensation. Such Award was challenged by the First Petitioner by filing Writ Petition. The order in the Writ Petition was of reinstatement but without back-wages. The Jal Nigam filed Special Leave Petition against the common order of the Single Bench. The Special Leave Petitions were decided on the basis of office order wherein it was resolved that in future, as and when any vacancy arises on daily wages/muster roll, the preference will be given to terminated/retrenched employee of the department.

Held, while dismissing the appeals:

i. The order had been passed on the basis of concession given on behalf of the workmen in light of the circular. There was no order of this Court to re-engage the workmen who were parties in the Special Leave Petitions. Therefore, in the absence of any specific and categorical direction of reinstatement, the Petitioners could not claim any right for reinstatement on the basis of the orders passed by this Court.

ii. The Order of this Court was to take workmen on daily wage basis as per office order. The argument that they accepted the order under the impression that the workmen were being reinstated could not be accepted as the order had been passed on the basis of the circular which contemplates that the workmen shall be reinstated as per the seniority list as and when requirement in future arises. The Order of the Court could not be interpreted on the basis of the impressions which may be drawn by the Petitioners, in view of the specific order passed by this Court.

iii. The argument that Group D posts were available against which Petitioners may be appointed was not tenable. The Group D posts were required to be filled on the basis of qualifications prescribed for filling up of such posts in the Rules as may be applicable to make appointments to such posts. The Petitioners, if eligible, could compete for such appointments. But merely they were once engaged on muster roll, they could not have right to seek regular appointment against Group D posts dehors the eligibility conditions prescribed in the Rules. The regular appointment can be made keeping in view the principles of public appointment which was by issuance of an advertisement giving opportunity to all eligible candidates to apply and to consider their suitability for the posts in non-discriminatory manner. The Petitioners appointed on muster roll basis could not claim regular appointment against the vacant Group D posts when the Award of the Labour Court was of reinstatement and not that of regular appointment.

iv. Petitioners could not claim any grievance of not engaging them in pursuance of the order passed by this Court when this Court had disposed of the Special Leave Petitions in the light of circular which contemplates that the retrenched employees would be re-engaged in case any requirement arises and in order of seniority. Therefore, it could not be said that the Respondents had violated any order passed by this Court.

NINE

BIHAR STATE BEVERAGES CORPORATION LTD. AND ORS. VS. NARESH KUMAR MISHRA AND ORS., 2019

Hon'ble Judges/Coram:

L. Nageswara Rao and M.R. Shah, JJ.

Equivalent Citation: AIR2019SC1051, 2019(2)BLJ355, 2021(I)CLR37, [2020(164)FLR661], 2019(1)J.L.J.R.512, 2019LabIC1179, 2019(4)LLN20(SC), 2019(1)PLJR584, 2019(2)SCALE509, (2019)5SCC110, (2019)1SCC(LS)747, 2019 (5) SCJ 595, 2019(1)SCT789(SC), 2019(1)SLJ470(SC), (2019)4WBLR(SC)105, MANU/SC/0142/2019

Relevant sections: Section 617 of the Companies Act; Rule 282 and 283 of the Bihar Service Code

Number of pages in original Judgment: 08

Case Note:

Service - Pay scale - Revision of - Respondents-employees were working with Appellant Corporation on different posts -Employees working with Corporation were denied benefit of pay scale as per the recommendations of sixth Pay Revision Committee - Respondents preferred writ petitions before

High Court for appropriate direction to Corporation to grant them pay scale of sixth Pay Revision Committee - Single Judge dismissed petitions - Feeling aggrieved with judgment and order of Single Judge, Respondents preferred appeal - Division Bench had allowed appeal and quashed and set aside judgment and order passed by Single Judge - Division Bench also directed Corporation to pay revision of pay scales in terms of sixth Pay Revision Committee - Hence, present appeal - Whether Respondents wree entitled for pay scales in terms of sixth Pay Revision Committee.

Brief Facts:

The Appellant Corporation issued an Advertisement for making appointment by way of contract/deputation of the employees of other Board and Corporation and also from the retired employees of the Board and/ or Corporation of the State or Central Government. The Respondents employees applied pursuant to the aforesaid advertisement. All of them were selected on various posts in the Corporation. The employees working with the Corporation were denied the benefit of the pay scale as per the recommendations of the sixth Pay Revision Committee. Thereafter, the Board of the Corporation in its meeting passed a resolution and it was resolved that all those employees working with the Appellant Corporation on deputation shall be paid the pay scale payable in their parent Corporation and deputation allowance. Therefore, the Respondents preferred the writ petitions before the High Court for an appropriate direction to the Corporation to grant them the pay scale of sixth Pay Revision Committee. The Single Judge dismissed petitions preferred by Respondents. Feeling aggrieved and dissatisfied with the judgment and order of the Single Judge dismissing the writ petitions, Respondents preferred the Letters Patent Appeal. The Division Bench had allowed appeal and directed the Corporation to follow the Principle of Equal wages for equal work in the matter of grant of pay scale. The Division Bench also directed the Corporation to pay the revision of pay scales in terms of the sixth Pay Revision Committee and resolution of the Board of Directors.

Held, while dismissing the appeal:

i. So far as the quashing and setting aside the resolution by which the Corporation resolved to pay salary to the employees of the Corporation as was being paid in the parent Board/parent organization was concerned, it was required to be noted that it was not in dispute that the respective original Writ Petitioners were on deputation from different Boards/Organizations. Therefore, if the resolution was permitted to be implemented, in that case, there shall be disparity in the pay scale/salary of the employees of the Corporation doing the same/similar work. There may be different pay scales/salaries in the respective parent organizations. However, when they were working with the Corporation and doing the similar work, they had to be paid the salary which is paid to other employees doing the same/similar work. It was not in dispute that the employees working on different posts in the Corporation were doing the same/similar work. Therefore, the Division Bench of the High Court had rightly applied the Principle of Equal Pay for Equal Work and had rightly quashed and set aside the resolution.

ii. So far as the impugned judgment and order passed by the High Court directing the Appellant Corporation to grant pay scale to the Respondents as per the sixth PRC was concerned, it was required to be noted that, as such, the Appellant Corporation itself took a conscious decision to grant the benefit of sixth PRC to the employees working with the Corporation. However, on the advice of the Finance Department that the Corporation may grant the benefit of sixth PRC to their permanent employees and not to the employees on deputation, the Corporation thereafter took a decision not to grant the benefit of the pay scale as per the sixth PRC. As rightly held by the Division Bench of the High Court, the advice by the Finance Department was non-application of mind, inasmuch so far as the Corporation was concerned, there was not a single employee appointed by the Corporation on permanent basis and the entire staff was either on deputation or on contract basis from other Boards/organizations. Therefore, the Division Bench of the High Court has rightly directed the Appellant Corporation to grant the pay scale to the Respondents as per the sixth PRC. However, at the same time, it was to be clarified that they would get the pay scale as per the sixth PRC so long as they continue to work with the Appellant Corporation and as and when they were repatriated, in that case, they shall be governed by the pay scale paid to the employees in the parent Board/Organization.

PPP

TEN

PREM SINGH VS. STATE OF UTTAR PRADESH AND ORS., 2019

Hon'ble Judges/Coram:

Arun Mishra, S. Abdul Nazeer and M.R. Shah, JJ.

Equivalent Citation: AIR2019SC4390, 2020 (139) ALR 195, 2019 6 AWC5480SC, 2019(3)ESC801(SC), [2020(164)FLR671], (2019)6MLJ741, 2019(12)SCALE20, (2019)10SCC516, (2020)1SCC(LS)1, 2019 (9) SCJ 584, 2019(4)SCT386(SC), 2019(3)SLJ233(SC), 2020(1)SLR286(SC), (2019)4UPLBEC3014, MANU/SC/1197/2019

Relevant sections: Rule3(8) of U.P. Retirement Benefit Rules, 1961

Number of pages in original Judgment: 20

Case Note:

Service - Grant of pension - Rule 3(8) of U.P. Retirement Benefit Rules, 1961 - Issue in present case was relating validity of to Rule 3(8) of Rules of 1961 and Regulation 370 of the Civil Services Regulation of Uttar Pradesh due to fact that, this Court has upheld decision regarding pari materia provision enacted in the State of Punjab which excluded computation of period of work-charged services from qualifying service for pension - Present Court had affirmed decision of High Court of State of Punjab and Haryana rendered in Kesar Singh v. State of Punjab - Whether services rendered in the work-charged establishment shall be treated as qualifying service for grant of pension

Brief Facts:

The Appellant was appointed as a Welder in the year 1965 in a work-charged establishment. He was transferred from one place to another and thereafter ultimately the Selection Committee recommended for regularization of his services. His services were regularized on 13.3.2002 and was posted as Pump Operator in the pay scale of Rs. 3050-4590 in the regular establishment. He superannuated on 31.1.2007. Then he filed a writ petition in the High Court to count period spent in the work-charged establishment as qualifying service under the Rules of 1965. The High Court directed to submit a representation, accordingly it was filed which met with rejection. Yet another representation filed also met with the same fate vide order. The writ petition and special appeal had been dismissed.

Held, while allowing the appeal:

i. The qualifying service is the one which is in accordance with the provisions of Regulation 368 i.e. holding a substantive post on a permanent establishment. The proviso to Rule 3(8) clarify that continuous, temporary or officiating service followed without interruption by confirmation in the same or any other post is also included in the qualifying service except in the case of periods of temporary and officiating service in a non-pensionable establishment. The service in work-charged establishment and period of service in a post paid from contingencies shall also not count as qualifying service.
ii. The Note appended to Rule 3(8) contains a provision that, if the service is rendered in a non-pensionable establishment, work-charged establishment or in a post paid from contingencies, falls between two periods of temporary service in a pensionable establishment or between a period of temporary service and permanent service in a pensionable establishment, it will not constitute an interruption of service. Thus, note contains a clear provision to count the qualifying service rendered in work-charged, contingency paid and non-pensionable establishment to be counted towards pensionable service, in the exigencies provided therein.
iii. The provisions contained in Regulation 370 of the Civil Services Regulations excludes service in a non-pensionable establishment, work-charged establishment and in a post paid from contingencies from the purview of qualifying service. Under Regulation 361 of the Civil Services Regulations, the services must be under the Government and the employment must be substantive and permanent basis.

iv. It would depend upon the service Rules or schemes whether the period of work-charged service has to be counted for ACP, in case provision has been made under a particular statute, Rule or scheme, service rendered as work-charged employees can be counted. It would depend upon the relevant provision of which benefit is claimed. Again, this Court has emphasized that by its very nature of employment work-charged employees have not to continue for long, employment comes to an end with the project.

v. The question arises whether the imposition of rider that such service to be counted has to be rendered in-between two spells of temporary or temporary and permanent service is legal and proper. Once regularization had been made on vacant posts, though the employee had not served prior to that on temporary basis, considering the nature of appointment, though it was not a regular appointment, it was made on monthly salary and thereafter in the pay scale of work-charged establishment the efficiency bar was permitted to be crossed. It would be highly discriminatory and irrational because of the rider contained in Note to Rule 3(8) of 1961 Rules, not to count such service particularly, when it can be counted, in case such service is sandwiched between two temporary or in-between temporary and permanent services. There is no rhyme or reason not to count the service of work-charged period in case it has been rendered before regularisation. An impermissible classification has been made under Rule 3(8). It would be highly unjust, impermissible and irrational to deprive such employees benefit of the qualifying service. Service of work-charged period remains the same for all the employees, once it is to be counted for one class, it has to be counted for all to prevent discrimination. The classification cannot be done on the irrational basis and when Respondents are themselves counting period spent in such service, it would be highly discriminatory not to count the service on the basis of flimsy classification. The rider put on that work-charged service should have preceded by temporary capacity is discriminatory and irrational and creates an impermissible classification.

vi. As it would be unjust, illegal and impermissible to make aforesaid classification to make the Rule 3(8) valid and non discriminatory, present Court has read down the provisions of Rule 3(8) and hold that services rendered even prior to regularisation in the capacity of work-charged employees, contingency paid fund employees or non-pensionable establishment shall also be counted towards the qualifying service even if such service is not preceded by temporary or regular appointment in a pensionable establishment.

vii. In view of the note appended to Rule 3(8), the provision contained in Regulation 370 of the Civil Services Regulations has to be struck down as also the instructions contained in Para 669 of the Financial Handbook.

viii. There are some of the employees who have not been regularized in spite of having rendered the services for 30-40 or more years whereas they have been superannuated. As they have worked in the work-charged establishment, not against any particular project, their services ought to have been regularized under the Government instructions and even as per the decision of this Court in Secretary, State of Karnataka and Ors. v. Uma Devi. This Court in the said decision has laid down that, in case services have been rendered for more than ten years without the cover of the Court's order, as one time measure, the services be regularized of such employees. In the facts of the case, those employees who have worked for ten years or more should have been regularized. It would not be proper to regulate them for consideration of regularisation as others have been regularised, we direct that their services be treated as a regular one. However, it is made clear that they shall not be entitled to claiming any dues of difference in wages had they been continued in service regularly before attaining the age of superannuation. They shall be entitled to receive the pension as if they have retired from the regular establishment and the services rendered by them right from the day they entered the work-charged establishment shall be counted as qualifying service for purpose of pension.

ix. In view of reading down Rule 3(8) of the U.P. Retirement Benefits Rules, 1961, present Court held that, services rendered in the work-charged establishment shall be treated as qualifying service under the aforesaid Rule for grant of pension. The arrears of pension shall be confined to three years only before the date of the order. Resultantly, the appeals filed by the employees are allowed and filed by the State are dismissed.

PPP

ELEVEN

State of Bihar and Ors. Vs. The Bihar Secondary Teachers Struggle Committee, Munger and Ors., 2019

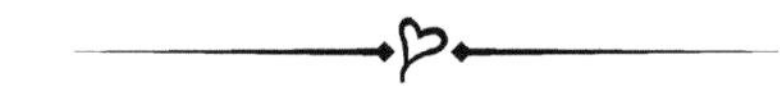

Hon'ble Judges/Coram:

Abhay Manohar Sapre and U.U. Lalit, JJ.

Equivalent Citation: AIR2019SC2521, 2019(3)ALT292, 2019(3)BLJ358, 2019(2)ESC558(SC), 2019(2)J.L.J.R.441, 2019LabIC2773, (2019)5MLJ560, 2019(2)PLJR454, 2019(8)SCALE124, (2019)18SCC301, 2019(3)SCT245(SC), 2019(2)SLJ278(SC), MANU/SC/0748/2019.

Relevant sections: Articles 21A and 243 of Constitution of India, 1950

Number of pages in original Judgment: 59

Ratio Decidendi:

Granting pay scales is a purely executive function and hence the court should not interfere with the same

Case Note:

Service - Pay scale - Parity thereto - Articles 21A and 243 of Constitution of India, 1950 - Appeal was against impugned order of High Court observing that, action on part of State in denying pay-scales to Niyojit Teachers was arbitrary and unreasonable - Whether Niyojit Teachers were right in their submission that, they were entitled to and were rightly granted 'equal pay for equal work' - Whether State was justified in its approach and was right in claiming that, distinction made by it was correct and fair.

Brief Facts:

In 1981, all non-Government Secondary Schools were nationalized and the management was taken over by State of Bihar. Consequently, all teaching and non-teaching staff were given salaries and emoluments at the Government scales. With the schemes like Sarva Shiksha Abhiyan, introduction of Article 21A in the Constitution and coming into force of the Right of Children to Free and Compulsion Education Act, 2009 ('RTE Act'), the State was required to induct large number of teachers in order to meet the required obligations. These teachers employed at Panchayat, Nagar Panchayat and Municipal levels were not given same salaries and emoluments like the teachers who were paid at the Government scales. The petitions seeking same salaries and emoluments on the principle of "equal pay for equal work" filed by the latter category of teachers, were allowed by the High Court. The view taken by the High Court is presently under challenge at the instance of the State. It was found that the admitted position was that both categories of teachers were discharging similar duties of imparting instructions in same schools and were having necessary qualifications as were possessed by the teachers appointed before 2006. Niyojit Teachers are regular teachers working in the nationalised school under the control of the State Government. The State Government has adopted two different pay-scales one for the Niyojit Shikshak and the other for the teachers known as regular teachers appointed prior to framing of 2006 Rules. Such discrimination in the pay-scale on the basis of artificial distinction is unreasonable.

Held, while allowing the appeal:

i. In the year 2002 itself, Scheme known as Sarva Shiksha Abhiyan was introduced at the Central level. In terms of the Scheme, the facilities of education and infrastructure were required to be spread through the length and breadth of the respective States. The steps taken in that behalf, specially in the present matter, indicate that sometime in 2002 more than one lakh Shiksha Mitras were appointed by the State. These Shiksha Mitras were not part of the regular cadre of Government Teachers, were not appointed through the regular process of selection and their services were engaged on a fixed salary. These Shiksha Mitras, who were outside the regular cadre of teachers, were entrusted with the job of manning schools in the remotest corners of the State. Sometime in 2006, certain decisions were taken by the Cabinet of Ministers, Government of Bihar. The control in respect of appointment of teachers in all nationalized schools and other aspects, which were hitherto before with the State Government, were given over to various Panchayat Raj institutions. This was in conformity with Articles 243G read with Serial No. 17 of the Eleventh Schedule in respect of Panchayats at the village, intermediate and at district levels and also in terms of Article 243W read with Serial No. 13 of the Twelfth Schedule in respect of Nagar Panchayats, Municipal Councils or Municipal Corporations. The decisions taken by the Cabinet were in accord with the constitutional mandate of enabling Panchayat Raj Systems on one hand while on the other, the decision also raised the number of teachers substantially so that national parameters on student: teacher ratio could be achieved by the State.

ii. The doctrine of 'equal pay for equal work' is not an abstract doctrine. The principle of 'equal pay for equal work' has no mechanical application in every case. The very fact that the person has not gone through the process of recruitment may itself, in certain cases, makes a difference. The application of the principle of 'equal pay for equal work' requires consideration of various dimensions of a given job. Thus, normally the applicability of this principle must be left to be evaluated and determined by an expert body. These are not matters where a writ court can lightly interfere. Granting pay scales is a purely executive function and hence the court should not interfere with the same. It may have a cascading effect creating all kinds of problems for the Government and authorities. Equation of posts and salary is a complex matter which should be left to an expert body. Granting of pay parity by the court may result in a cascading effect and reaction which can have adverse consequences. Before entertaining and accepting the claim based on the principle of equal pay for equal work, the Court must consider the factors like the source and mode of recruitment/appointment. In a given case, mode of selection may be considered as one of the factors which may make a difference.

iii. Even, when the teachers from both the cadres were discharging similar duties and responsibilities, the decision of the State government to maintain different identities of these two cadres was not found objectionable by this Court and further there could be inter se distinctions between these two cadres. It is true that, both the cadres were enjoying same pay structure but the submission that the chances of promotion ought to be similar was not accepted by the Court.

iv. It was open to the State to have two distinct cadres namely that of 'Government Teachers' and 'Niyojit Teachers' with Government Teachers being a dying or vanishing cadre. The incidents of these two cadres could be different. The idea by itself would not be discriminatory. The pay structure given to the Niyojit Teachers was definitely lower than what was given to Government Teachers but the number of Government Teachers was considerably lower than the number of Niyojit Teachers. Presently there are just about 66,000 Government Teachers in the State as against nearly 4 lakh Niyojit Teachers. There is scope for further appointment of about 1 lakh teachers which could mean that as against 5 lakh teachers the number of State Teachers would progressively be going down. The parity that is claimed is by the larger group with the lesser group as stated above which itself is a dying or a vanishing cadre. The mode of recruitment of Niyojit Teachers is completely different from that of the Government Teachers as stated above.

v. It is true that, the budgetary constraints or financial implications can never be a ground, if there is violation of Fundamental Rights of a citizen. Similarly, while construing the provisions of the RTE Act and the Rules framed thereunder, that interpretation ought to be accepted which would make the Right available under Article 21A a reality. As the text of the Article shows the provision is essentially child-centric. There cannot be two views as regards the point that Free and Compulsory Education ought to be quality education. However, such premise cannot lead to the further conclusion that in order to have quality education, Niyojit Teachers ought to be paid emoluments at the same level as are applicable to the State Teachers. The modalities in which expert teachers can be found, whether by giving them better scales and/or by insisting on threshold ability which could be tested through examinations such as TET Examination are for the Executive to consider.

vi. There has been no violation of the Rights of the Niyojit Teachers nor has there been any discrimination against them. Efforts on part of the State Government could not be labelled as unfair or discriminatory. The tabular charts placed on record by the State also show continuous improvements made by the State in the packages made available to the

Niyojit Teachers. Said attempts also show that the State is moving in the right direction and the gap which presently exists between the Government Teachers and the Niyojit Teachers would progressively get diminished. Considering the large number of Niyojit Teachers as against the Government Teachers, the steps taken by the State as evident from various tabular charts presented by it are in the right direction. At this juncture, any directions as have been passed by the High Court, may break even tempo which the State has consistently been able to achieve.

vii. The teachers must be entitled to decent emoluments. The State may consider raising the scales of Niyojit Teachers at least to the level suggested by the Committee, without insisting on any test or examination advised by the Committee. Those who clear such test or examination, may be given even better scales. Appeals allowed.

ÞÞÞ

TWELVE

THE STATE BANK OF INDIA AND ORS. VS. RAVINDRA NATH AND ORS., 2019

Hon'ble Judges/Coram:

U.U. Lalit and Hemant Gupta, JJ.

Equivalent Citation: 2019(3)ABR208, AIR2019SC1405, 2019(2)ALLMR955, 2019(2)J.L.J.R.120, 2019LabIC1535, 2019(3)LLN549(SC), 2019(2)PLJR131, 2019(3)SCALE350, (2019)5SCC612, 2019(2)SCT81(SC), (2019)1UPLBEC596, MANU/SC/0184/2019

Relevant sections: Section 18 of State Bank of India Act, 1955

Number of pages in original Judgment: 06

Case Note:

Service - Reduction in salary - Section 18 of State Bank of India Act, 1955 - Challenge in present appeal was to an Order passed by High Court, whereby communication dated 16th January, 2001 re-fixing salary of Respondent from 1st January, 2001 was set aside - Whether salary had been fixed for all Officers of Public Sector Banks in a non-discriminatory manner.

Brief Facts:

Respondent-writ Petitioner before High Court joined Appellant Bank in year 1981. After almost nineteen years vide letter dated 24th June, 2000, he was posted at Johannesburg Branch (South Africa) as Manager (Credit) as a Scale V Officer on a fixed salary of US $ 1965 (net) per month but subject to change from time to time. Apart from such salary, Respondent was granted various allowances including reimbursement of education expenses of children, usage of Bank's car, leave and reimbursement of medical expenses apart from host of other allowances. There was also a condition that, salary and terms and conditions as spelt out in letter were subject to review and revision by Bank from time to time. It was on 16th January, 2001, salary in respect of Respondent was re-fixed as US $ 1300 w.e.f. 1st January, 2001. Same was subsequently revised to US $ 1380 on 14th December, 2001. It was stand of Bank that when Respondent was sent to Johannesburg, salary was fixed on Consumer Price Index of 1992 on basis of directives of Working Group of Standing Committee w.e.f. 1st January, 1995 in absence of availability of Cost of Living Index. But since, relevant data became available in March 2000, Working Group in its meeting held on 15th January, 2001, had re-fixed salary on basis of formula approved by Standing Committee. High Court in impugned judgment held that, Respondent-writ Petitioner had no privity to contract with Standing Committee on basis of which salary was reduced. It had also held that, salary of Respondent had been reduced within three months which was unfair and arbitrary and that letter dated 24th June, 2000 did not even remotely suggest that salary of US $ 1965 was tentative, nor available information taken into consideration for fixing salary was shared with Respondent.

Held, while allowing the appeal:

i. A perusal of relevant service conditions showed that, salary of US $ 1965 was not promised to be paid for entire period of posting in Johannesburg. It was subject to change either way that was increase or decrease. Bank had explained that, such salary of US $ 1965 was fixed in absence of Cost of Living Index on basis of recommendations of Committee. Later, Standing Committee was constituted in exercise of the powers under Section 18 of Act mandating that, any change in future in salaries and perquisites and other service conditions had to be affected with prior approval of Standing Committee.
ii. It was in view of such directions that, Appellant Bank framed service conditions and allied matters. It was thereafter on 15th January, 2001, Working Group of Standing Committee decided salary payable to Officers of Bank. Such salary structure was meant for all Officers of Public Sector Banks posted abroad. Such recommendations were applicable in non-discriminatory manner to all Officers of Public Sector

Banks.

iii. Salary was reduced from month of January, 2001, though, Respondent-writ Petitioner had joined only on 21stSeptember, 2000. Respondent never offered to seek repatriation to India and in fact sought voluntary retirement on depositing of Rs. 10,00,000 for further stay in Johannesburg. It showed that, there was no financial loss suffered by him on account of reduction in salary, but actually, he found it lucrative to resign from service of Bank and to stay in Johannesburg after payment of substantial amount of Rs. 10,00,000.

iv. Salary had been fixed in terms of directions of Government of India, in respect of all Public Sector Banks keeping in view the Cost of Living Index in different countries and making adjustments in salaries according to Cost of Living of each country. Cost of Living in each country was separate and distinct and such factors had been taken into consideration while fixing salary on basis of Bulletin of Statistics published by U.N. in March, 2000. Earlier fixation of salary for Johannesburg was fixed by Working Group w.e.f. 1st January, 1995 on basis of Consumer Price Index of 1992 as per International Financial, Statistics (IMF Publication-September, 1995). Revised salary structure was not meant for any particular official but was applicable to all Officers of Public Sector Banks posted abroad.

v. Bulletin of Statistics published by U.N. in March, 2000 was considered by Standing Committee in its meeting held on 15.01.2001. Respondent was informed of his reduced salary very next day. Therefore, Cost of Living Index on basis of March, 2000 Report was considered in January, 2001. Such decision could not be said to be arbitrary only because it was taken after about nine months of publication of data.

vi. Reasoning given by High Court that, there was no privity of contract of Respondent-writ Petitioner with Standing Committee was not tenable. Respondent-writ Petitioner as an Officer of Bank was bound by salary structure approved by Bank for its Officers. Decision of Standing Committee was a part of decision-making in respect of salary payable to employees of Banks. Employee of a Bank had no right that, he should be associated with decision-making process in respect of fixation of salary. However, if question of reasonableness of salary arose, then in exercise of power of judicial review, Court might examine decision-making process. In exercise of power of judicial review, there was no infirmity in decision of Standing Committee taken on 15th January, 2001 in pursuance to direction of Government of India issued under Section 18 of Act.

vii. Since, salary had been fixed for all Officers of Public Sector Banks in a non-discriminatory manner keeping in view Cost of Living Index, High Court erred in law in setting aside reduction in salary. There was reasonable basis of reduction of salary. Still further there was no promise ever made to Respondent-writ Petitioner that, his salary of US $ 1965 shall remain unchanged during period of his posting. In fact, it was categorically mentioned that, salary as well as perquisites were subject to change from time to time. Therefore, mere fact that, salary was changed subsequently, it would not confer any legally enforceable right in favour of Respondent to challenge same on ground that, same was arbitrary or unjust.

viii. Order passed by High Court was set aside. Appeal allowed.

PPP

THIRTEEN

STEEL AUTHORITY OF INDIA LTD. AND ORS. VS. JAGGU AND ORS., 2019

Hon'ble Judges/Coram:

A.M. Khanwilkar and Ajay Rastogi, JJ.

Equivalent Citation: AIR2019SC3601, 2019(6)ALT143, 2019(5)BLJ137, 2019(III)CLR165, 2019(3)ESC641(SC), [2019(162)FLR913], 2019(3)JLJ252, (2019)IIILLJ257SC, 2020(1)LLN278(SC), 2019(9)SCALE164, (2019)7SCC658, (2019)2SCC(LS)444, 2019 (8) SCJ 173, 2019(3)SCT339(SC), 2019(2)SLJ420(SC), 2019(5)SLR246(SC), 2019 (3) WLN 82 (SC), MANU/SC/0882/2019

Relevant sections: Sections 7, 8, 9, 10 and 12 of Contract Labour (Regulation And Abolition) Act, 1970; Section 20(1) of Minimum Wages Act, 1948

Number of pages in original Judgment: 14

Case Note:

Labour And Industrial - Payment of wages - Parity thereto - Sections 7, 8, 9, 10 and 12 of Contract Labour (Regulation And Abolition) Act, 1970 (CLRA Act) and Section 20(1) of Minimum Wages Act, 1948 - Appeal was against impugned order of High Court directing a consolidated sum of Rs. 5 crore to be paid towards compensation to aggrieved employees - Whether claim of the Respondents that, as they had discharged same or similar nature of work as that of direct employee of the establishment, it made them entitled for wages which are payable to an employee who was directly/regularly appointed in the establishment was sustainable.

Brief Facts:

Present appeals arise from the proceedings initiated by the workers under the Minimum Wages Act, 1948 who had been in employment after issuance of the prohibition notification dated 17th March 1993. Claim of the Respondents in their application filed under Section 20(1) of Act, 1948 was that, as they had discharged the same or similar nature of work as that of direct employee of the establishment, it makes them entitled for the wages which are payable to an employee who is directly/regularly appointed in the establishment to whom wages are paid in terms of NJCS memorandum of Agreement dated 30th July, 1975. The complaint of the Applicant Jaggu before the prescribed authority of which a reference has been made, appears to be that, the rates of wages of SAIL which were governed by various settlements/ agreements entered between the management and the registered Union of regular employees of SAIL are legally enforceable and the Applicant is also entitled to the wages and such other service benefits as per those settlements after a prohibition notification has been published by the appropriate Government under Section 10(1) of the CLRA Act. The prescribed authority after holding a summary enquiry as contemplated under the Act, 1948 under its Order allowed the claim petitions with five times of compensation in favour of 2040 contract employees who have been represented by Ispat Khadan Janta Mazdoor Union. The order of the Payment of Wages Authority came to be challenged by the Appellant SAIL by way of writ petition before the Single Judge of High Court which was partly allowed vide Order holding that the justice would be met, if the Respondents (employees) are allowed 6% interest on the amount payable to each of them as compensation from the date of passing of the impugned order of the authority till its payment. It was further challenged before the Division Bench of the High Court that, came to be dismissed vide impugned judgment with a modification that, instead of grant of 6% interest as compensation, a consolidated sum of Rs. 5 crore be paid towards compensation to the aggrieved employees, which is a subject matter of challenge in these appeals.

Held, while allowing the appeal:

i. CLRA Act is a complete code in itself and regulate the employment of contract labour in certain establishments and provide for its abolition in certain circumstances and for matters connected therewith. The title of the Act itself indicates that, the Act does not provide for total abolition of the contract labour, but only for its abolition in certain circumstances, and to regulate the employment of contract labour in the establishments which are registered under Section 7 and working through the contractors who are holding licence under Section 12 of the Act. Section 8 provides for the revocation of registration in certain cases and Section 9 provides the effect of non-registration. Section 10 is one of the back bone of the Act which provides for prohibition of employment of contract labour in any establishment.

ii. In the instant case, the establishment was duly registered under Section 7 of the Act and the contractor through whom the contract labour was engaged was holding its licence under Section 12 of the Act but in the changed circumstances, the appropriate Government took a decision to put a prohibition in making employment of contract labour in scheduled employment for various reasons which is not a subject matter of enquiry in the instant case and in consequence of the prohibition notification dated 17th March, 1993 published under Section 10(1) of the CLRA Act, the contract labour working in the establishment ceased to function and the contract between the principal employer and contractor stands extinguished.

iii. At the same time, an obligation to provide amenities conferred by the Act to the workers has been referred to under Chapter V of the CLRA Act and the primary responsibility is of a contractor that each worker employed by him as contract labour has to be paid his due wages before the expiry of such period as may be prescribed with an exception provided under Section 21(4) of the Act. In case the contractor fails to make payment of wages within the prescribed period or makes short payment, then the principal employer shall be liable to make payment of wages in full or the unpaid balance due, as the case may be, to the contract labour employed by the contractor and recover the amount so paid from the contractor under any of the methods prescribed by law.

iv. In the instant case, after issuance of the prohibition notification dated 17th March, 1993 under Section 10(1) of the CLRA Act having being published, provisions of the CLRA Act or CLRA Central Rules, 1971 framed thereunder would not be available to either of the party to strengthen its claim. Minimum wages as prayed for in the application filed by Respondents before the prescribed authority under Section 20(1) of the Act, 1948 could be claimed independently under Act, 1948 which undisputedly in the instant case was Rs. 11.65 per day over the minimum wages to be paid by the Appellant to each of the Respondent (2040 employees) in terms of the agreement executed between the parties and that was indeed complied with by the Appellants in its true spirit.

v. A mere assertion of fact that ,the contract labour which was allowed to continue after the prohibition notification came to be published dated 17th March, 1993 in the establishment of the Appellant SAIL performing same or similar kind of work in the establishment of the principal employer is not sufficient to endorse their entitlement of claiming wages notified by the NJCS memorandum of agreement for direct/regular employees of the establishment applicable universally to all the steel industries.

Order of the prescribed authority under the Act, 1948 and confirmed by the High Court are unsustainable. Appeal allowed.

PPP

FOURTEEN

DTC Security Staff Union Vs. DTC and Ors., 2018

Hon'ble Judges/Coram:

Ranjan Gogoi, R. Banumathi and Navin Sinha, JJ.

Equivalent Citation: 2018(3)BLJ143, 2018(II)CLR761, [2018(157)FLR987], 2018(2)LLN545(SC), 2018LLR1055, 2018(7)SCALE323, (2018)16SCC619, (2019)1SCC(LS)317, 2019 (1) SCJ 523, 2018(3)SCT83(SC), 2018(5)SLR131(SC), (2018)2UPLBEC1466, MANU/SC/0550/2018

Relevant sections: Industrial Disputes Act, 1947; Article 226 of the Constitution of India

Number of pages in original Judgment: 04

Case Note:

Labor and Industrial - Pay Scale - Revision - Present appeal filed against order wherein High Court set aside award passed by Tribunal thereby denying Appellant's entitlement to revision of pay scale - Whether order of High Court justifiable

Brief Facts:

The Appellant had sought a Reference with regard to revision of pay-scale of security staff up to the rank of assistant security inspector. The Industrial Tribunal passed an award in favor of the Appellant. On appeal the High Court set aside the award passed by the Tribunal thereby denying Appellant's entitlement to revision of pay scale. Hence, present appeal was filed.

Held, while dismissing the Appeal:

i. There was no material to hold that pay-scale of deputy security officer and security officer in the Corporation was consciously kept at par with that of the Delhi Police keeping in mind aspects with regard to the qualifications, nature of duties, etc. Merely because the pay-scale may have been and remained the same, it could not lead to the conclusion of a conscious parity on the principle of equal pay for equal work so as to make it discriminatory and a ground for grant of parity to assistant security officer, security havaldar and security guard also. The Tribunal ought to have refrained from going into the exercise of fixation of pay-scales no sooner that it was brought to its attention that a Commission constituted for the purpose was examining the same. Though the Tribunal examined the pay scales given to similarly situated security personnel in other organizations, and also the next below post principle in the Corporation itself, ignoring the difference in the methods of recruitment and qualifications for appointment in the two organizations, it primarily based its conclusion to grant parity of pay-scale to assistant security officer, security havaldar and security guard merely for the reason that parity of pay-scale existed for the posts of deputy security officer and security officer with that of the Delhi Police.

The pay-scale of the employees of the Corporation, including the security cadre, have been revised from time to time in accordance with the recommendations of 4th, 5th, 6th Pay-Commission and now the 7th Pay-Commission. There was no material on record that the Appellant at any time filed any objection or raised issues for grant of appropriate pay-scale either before the 4th Pay-Commission or the successive Commissions. If the award of the Tribunal was to be implemented, it would create a highly anomalous position in the Corporation, and should lead to serious complications with regard to the issues of pay-scale with regard to recommendations of the Pay-Commission and would generate further heartburn and related problems.

PPP

FIFTEEN

RAM NARESH RAWAT VS. ASHWINI RAY AND ORS., 2016

Hon'ble Judges/Coram:

A.K. Sikri and N.V. Ramana, JJ.

Equivalent Citation: 2016 (4) CCC 369 , 2017(I)CLR656, 2017(1)ESC22(SC), [2017(153)FLR601], 2017(1)J.L.J.R.329, (2017)ILLJ1SC, 2016(4)LLN557(SC), 2017(4)MhLj12, 2017(3)MPLJ20, 2017(2)PLJR1, 2016(12)SCALE816, (2017)3SCC436, (2017)1SCC(LS)646, 2017 (1) SCJ 571, 2017(2)SCT73(SC), 2017(2)SLR781(SC), MANU/SC/1598/2016

Relevant sections: Madhya Pradesh Industrial Environment (Standing Order) Rules, 1963

Number of pages in original Judgment: 13

Case Note:

Contempt of Court - Fixation of pay - Implementation of order - Madhya Pradesh Industrial Environment (Standing Order) Rules, 1963 - Petitioners were engaged by State as daily wagers - According to Petitioners, in terms of Rules, 1963, they became entitled to be classified as 'permanent employees' - However, their demand was not acceded to by State - Industrial dispute which resulted into award of labour court directing their classification as 'permanent' - Labour court also held that on their classification as permanent, they would be entitled to the pay-scale of permanent post - Unsuccessful appeals were filed by State - Resulted in passing of orders by concerned authorities in State Government classifying these Petitioners as permanent employees - It was also ordered that they shall be entitled to minimum pay as fixed by Labour Commission - Petitioners claimed that on their classification as 'permanent' to their respective posts they were entitled to receive pay-scale attached to said posts - These reliefs were granted to them by labour court - Appeal against to that before the industrial court and petition before High Court were also dismissed - Special leave petitions were filed which were dismissed by present Court - Petitioners were not satisfied with fixation and contended that pay fixation had not been done as per orders of present Court - Whether Petitioners were also entitled to increments - Whether Petitioner employees could be treated as 'regular' employees in view of their classification as 'permanent'

Brief Facts:

All the Petitioners, who filed contempt petitions, were engaged by the State on different dates on different posts but all of them were engaged as daily wagers. They continued as daily wagers for long spell of time. According to the Petitioners, in terms of Madhya Pradesh Industrial Environment (Standing Order) Rules, 1963, they became entitled to be classified as 'permanent employees'. However, their demand for classification as permanent employees was not acceded to by the State, which inaction of the State Government provoked some of these employees to raise the industrial dispute which resulted into award(s) of the labour court directing their classification as 'permanent'. The labour court also held that on their classification as permanent, they would be entitled to the pay-scale of permanent post from dates specified in the award. Appeals were filed by the State against those orders which were dismissed by the industrial court and writ petitions also came to be dismissed by the High Court. This resulted in passing of the orders by the concerned authorities in the State Government classifying these Petitioners as permanent employees. It was also ordered that they shall be entitled to minimum pay as fixed by the Labour Commission. This led to another round of litigation as the Petitioners claimed that on their classification as 'permanent' to their respective posts they were entitled to receive the pay-scale attached to the said posts. These reliefs were granted to them by the labour court against which appeal preferred before the industrial court and the writ petition before the High Court were also dismissed. In all these cases, thereafter, special leave petitions were filed which were dismissed by the present Court. The Petitioners were not satisfied with the fixation and contended that the pay fixation had not been done as per the orders of the present Court.

The precise submission was that once they were conferred the status of permanent employee by the court and it was also categorically held that they were entitled to regular pay attached to the said post, not only the pay should be fixed in the regular pay-scale, the Petitioners would also be entitled to the increments and other emoluments attached to the said post. In other words, they pleaded that fixation of pay at the minimum of the pay-scale is uncalled for and does not amount to complying with the directions of the Court in full measure. It was also submitted that in some other cases where the High Court has given similar directions, which are followed in their cases, the State Government has not only fixed pay in the regular pay-scale but has also been granting increments etc. as well.

Held, while dismissing the petition:

i. The matter was being examined in the contempt jurisdiction of the prsent Court. From the chronology of events given, it would be clear that initially these Petitioners had claimed their classification as 'permanent' to the respective posts. They succeeded in this attempt and the orders passed therein in their favour was that they would be classified as 'permanent' and that they would also be entitled to pay-scale of permanent posts from the dates specified in the award given by the labour court. In the second round of litigation, out of which present contempt petitions arise, direction of the High Court was to grant them pay-scales attached to the posts to which they are working. This order was upheld by the present Court as well inasmuch as Special Leave Petitions filed by the State Government have been dismissed by common orders. However, there was no specific direction for grant of increments. In order to implement the directions of High Court, against which special Leave Petitions have been dismissed, the State Government had passed order vide which the pay-scale of the Petitioners had been fixed in the pay-scale attached to these posts. This had also been given from the dates to which these Petitioners were held entitled to and on that basis arrears of pay have also been paid. However, the pay was fixed at the minimum of the said pay-scales and there is also stipulation in the said orders that these employees would not be entitled to increment of salary.

ii. The Petitioners had been given pay in the regular pay-scale. Petitioners, however, joined issue by contending that orders did not carry out the complete compliance of the directions given by the High Court that on fixation of pay in the regular pay-scale the Petitioners were also entitled to increments of salary, as is given to the regular employees, on annual basis.

iii. The Petitioners were initially engaged on daily wage basis. Their engagement was also done without following any selection procedure. It also does not emerge from record that the initial engagement of these Petitioners was against regular vacancies. Normally, in such a situation even if these persons, because of their long service and also on the assumption that they are discharging the same duties as discharged by regular employees, such employees can claim the salary which is being paid to regular employees holding similar posts on the principles of 'equal pay for equal work'. Even if principle of 'equal pay for equal work' is applicable, temporary employee shall be entitled to minimum of the pay-scale which is attached to the post, but without any increments.

iv. Merely by putting in six months' satisfactory service, an employee can be treated as 'permanent employee'. Rights which would flow to different categories of employees including 'permanent employee' are not stipulated in these Rules or even in the parent Act. It can be gathered from Rule 11 of the said Rules, which relates to termination of employment, that in case of a 'permanent employee' one month's notice or wages for one month in lieu of notice is required when the employment of a 'permanent employee' is to be terminated. On the other hand, no such notice or wages in lieu thereof is needed to be given to any other category of employees. Additional obligation casts on the employer is to record reasons for termination of service in writing and communicate the same to the employee.

v. A person who is known as 'permanent employee' would be treated as a regular employee but it did not appear to be exactly that kind of situation in the instant case when we find that merely after completing six months' service an employee gets right to be treated as 'permanent employee'. Moreover, the present Court drawn a distinction between 'permanent employee' and 'regular employee'.

vi. Though a 'permanent employee' has right to receive pay in the graded pay-scale, at the same time, he would be getting only minimum of the said pay-scale with no increments. It was only the regularisation in service which would entail grant of increments etc. in the pay-scale. There was no substance in the contentions raised by the Petitioners.

SIXTEEN

STATE OF PUNJAB VS. RAFIQ MASIH, 2014

Hon'ble Judges/Coram:

J.S. Khehar and Arun Mishra, JJ.

Equivalent Citation: AIR2015SC696, 2015(1)ALLMR(SC)957, 2015 (2) AWC 1570 (SC), 2015(1)CLJ(SC)192, 2015(I)CLR398, 2015(5)CTC455, [2015(145)FLR234], 2015(1)J.L.J.R.323, 2015(1)KLT429, 2015LabIC1743, (2015)1LLJ455SC, 2015(3)LLN575(SC), 2015-3-LW724, 2015(1)MPHT130, 2015(1)PLJR261, 2014(14)SCALE300, (2015)4SCC334, (2015)2SCC(LS)33, 2014 (10) SCJ 700, 2015(1)SCT195(SC), 2015(2)SLJ151(SC), 2016(8)SLR572(SC), MANU/SC/1195/2014

Relevant sections: Article 142, 14 to 18 of the Constitution of India

Number of pages in original Judgment: 11

Case Note:

Service - Excess monetary benefits - Entitlement thereto - All private Respondents were beneficiaries of mistake committed by employer, and on account of unintentional mistake, employees were in receipt of monetary benefits, beyond their due - Hence, present appeal - Whether all private Respondents, against whom order of recovery (of excess amount) had been made, could be exempted in law, from reimbursement of same to employees - Held, it would be justified to treat order of recovery, on account of wrongful payment made to employee, as arbitrary, if recovery was sought to be made after employee's retirement, or within one year of date of his retirement on superannuation - It was not possible to postulate all situations of hardship, which would govern employees on issue of recovery, where payments had mistakenly been made by employer, in excess of their entitlement -

Recoveries by employers, would be impermissible in law in cases of recovery from employees belonging to Class-III and Class-IV service, recovery from retired employees, or employees who were due to retire within one year, of order of recovery - Recovery from employees, when excess payment had been made for period in excess of five years, before order of recovery was issued - Recovery in cases where employee had wrongfully been required to discharge duties of higher post, and had been paid accordingly, even though he should have rightfully been required to work against inferior post - In any other case, where Court arrived at conclusion, that recovery if made from employee, would be iniquitous or harsh or arbitrary to such extent, as would far outweigh equitable balance of employer's right to recover - Hence, impugned orders passed by High Court quashing order of recovery upheld - Appeal disposed of.

Brief Facts:

All the private Respondents in the present bunch of cases, were given monetary benefits, which were in excess of their entitlement. These benefits flowed to them, consequent upon a mistake committed by the concerned competent authority, in determining the emoluments payable to them. The mistake could have occurred on account of a variety of reasons; including the grant of a status, which the concerned employee was not entitled to; or payment of salary in a higher scale, than in consonance of the right of the concerned employee; or because of a wrongful fixation of salary of the employee, consequent upon the upward revision of pay-scales; or for having been granted allowances, for which the concerned employee was not authorized. The long and short of the matter is, that all the private Respondents were beneficiaries of a mistake committed by the employer, and on account of the said unintentional mistake, employees were in receipt of monetary benefits, beyond their due.

Another essential factual component in this bunch of cases is, that the Respondent-employees were not guilty of furnishing any incorrect information, which had led the concerned competent authority, to commit the mistake of making the higher payment to the employees. The payment of higher dues to the private Respondents, in all these cases, was not on account of any misrepresentation made by them, nor was it on account of any fraud committed by them. Any participation of the private Respondents, in the mistake committed by the employer, in extending the undeserved monetary benefits to the Respondent-employees, is totally ruled out. It would therefore not be incorrect to record, that the private Respondents, were as innocent as their employers, in the wrongful determination of their inflated emoluments.

Held,

It is not possible to postulate all situations of hardship, which would govern employees on the issue of recovery, where payments have mistakenly been made by the employer, in excess of their entitlement. Be that as it may, based on the decisions referred to herein above, we may, as a ready reference, summarise the following few situations, wherein recoveries by the employers, would be impermissible in law:

i. Recovery from employees belonging to Class-III and Class-IV service (or Group 'C' and Group 'D' service).
ii. Recovery from retired employees, or employees who are due to retire within one year, of the order of recovery.
iii. Recovery from employees, when the excess payment has been made for a period in excess of five years, before the order of recovery is issued.
iv. Recovery in cases where an employee has wrongfully been required to discharge duties of a higher post, and has been paid accordingly, even though he should have rightfully been required to work against an inferior post.
v. In any other case, where the Court arrives at the conclusion, that recovery if made from the employee, would be iniquitous or harsh or arbitrary to such an extent, as would far outweigh the equitable balance of the employer's right to recover.

We are informed by the learned Counsel representing the Appellant-State of Punjab, that all the cases in this bunch of appeals, would undisputedly fall within the first four categories delineated hereinabove. In the appeals referred to above, therefore, the impugned orders passed by the High Court of Punjab and Haryana (quashing the order of recovery), shall be deemed to have been upheld, for the reasons recorded above. The appeals are disposed of in the above terms.

SEVENTEEN

NATIONAL ALUMINIUM COMPANY LTD. AND ORS. VS. ANANTA KISHORE ROUT AND ORS., 2014

Hon'ble Judges/Coram:

S.S. Nijjar and A.K. Sikri, JJ.

Equivalent Citation: 2014vii AD (S.C.) 669, 2014 (4) AWC 3457 (SC), 2014(II)CLR549, 118(2014)CLT109(SC), [2014(142)FLR643], 2014(3)J.L.J.R.57, JT2014(6)SC153, 2014LabIC2790, (2014)6MLJ115(SC), 2014(II)OLR83, 2014(II)OLR(SC)83, 2014(6)SCALE540, (2014)6SCC7556, (2014)6SCC756, (2014)2SCC(LS)353, 2014 (6) SCJ 328, 2014(3)SCT675(SC), 2014(4)SLR483(SC), MANU/SC/0431/2014

Relevant sections: Article 39(d) of the Constitution of India

Number of pages in original Judgment: 12

Case Note:

Constitution of India - Article 39(d)--Employment--Equal pay for equal work--Applicability--Employees of schools set up by N.A.L.C.O. not entitled to pay scale which are given to other employees of N.A.L.C.O.--As there cannot be comparison between two--Principle of 'equal pay for equal work' is not attracted at all--Those employees directly employed by N.A.L.C.O. discharging altogether different kinds of duties--Main activity of N.A.L.C.O.

is manufacture and production of alumina and aluminium--Process and method of recruitment of those employees, their eligibility conditions for appointment, nature of job done by those employees etc. is entirely different from employees of schools set up by N.A.L.C.O.--No parity in nature of work, mode of appointment, experience educational qualifications between N.A.L.C.O. employees and employees of schools set up by N.A.L.C.O.--Impugned judgment of High Court--Unsustainable and set aside.

Brief Facts:

The Appellant herein, National Aluminium Company Limited (NALCO) has established two schools for the benefit of the wards of its-employees. These schools are known as Saraswati Vidya Mandir (SVM) and located at NALCO Nagar in Angul district and at Damanjodi in Koraput district, Orissa. Management of these schools is presently in the hand of Saraswati Vidya Mandir (SVS) which is affiliated to Vidya Bharati Akhila Bharatiya Sikhya Sansthan.

Two Writ Petitions were filed by the employees of each of school in the Orissa High Court, Cuttack for a declaration that they are the employees of NALCO and be treated as such, with consequential prayer that these employees be also accorded suitable pay scales as admissible to the employees of NALCO. Having regard to the commonality of fact, situation under which these writ petitions were filed, as well as singularity of the issue involved, both these writ petitions were heard together by the High Court, the outcome of which is the judgment dated 21st December, 2006. The High Court has accepted the case of these employees of SVM holding them to be the employees of the NALCO. As a sequittor, direction is issued to the NALCO to make available the benefits, which are enjoyed by other employees of the NALCO. Present appeals, filed by NALCO, question the validity of the aforesaid judgment of the High Court.

Held, while allowing the petition:

We say at the cost of repetition that there is no parity in the nature of work, mode of appointment, experience, educational qualifications between the NALCO employees and the employees of the two schools. In fact, such a comparison can be made with their counter parts in the Government schools and/or aided or unaided schools. On that parameter, there cannot be any grievance of the staff which is getting better emoluments and enjoying far superior service conditions.

We thus, are of the opinion that the impugned judgment of the High Court is un-sustainable. Allowing these appeals, the judgment of the High

Court is hereby set aside. There shall, however, be no order as to costs.

EIGHTEEN

HUKAM CHAND GUPTA VS. DIRECTOR GENERAL, I.C.A.R. AND ORS., 2012

Hon'ble Judges/Coram:

S.S. Nijjar and H.L. Gokhale, JJ.

Equivalent Citation: AIR2013SC547, 2013(1)AJR701, 2012(6)ALLMR971, 2012(6)ALLMR(SC)971, 2013 1 AWC226SC, 2012(5)ESC738(SC), 2013LabIC275, MANU/SC/0977/2012

Relevant sections: Article 14, 16 and 39(d) of the Constitution of India

Number of pages in original Judgment: 07

Case Note:

Constitution of India--Articles 14, 16 and 39D--Employment--Revised pay scale--Assured Career Progression (A.C.P.) Scheme--Introduced in I.C.A.R. making necessary provision in statutory Service Rules--Admittedly, Madan given benefit under A.C.P. Scheme--Decision taken by respondent--Was within purview of Service Rules--And cannot be said to be arbitrary--Hence, claim made by appellant clearly misconceived--No merit in contention that there can be no distinction in pay scales between employees working at Headquarters--And employees working at institutional level--Employees working at Headquarters--Governed by completely different set of rules--Even hierarchy of posts and channels of promotion--Different--Similarity of nomenclature of two posts at Headquarters and institutional level--Would not necessarily require that pay scales of two posts should also be same--Prescription of two different pay scale--Would not violate principle of equal pay for equal work--Such action not arbitrary or violative of Articles 14, 16 and 39D--No merit in appeal.

The Assured Career Progression (A.C.P.) Scheme was introduced in the I.C.A.R. by making the necessary provision in the statutory Service Rules. Admittedly, Shri J.I.P. Madan has been given the benefit under the A.C.P. Scheme. Therefore, the decision taken by the respondent was within the purview of the Service Rules and cannot be said to be arbitrary. That being so, the claim made by the appellant is clearly misconceived.

The submission of appellant cannot be accepted that there can be no distinction in the pay scales between the employees working at Headquarters and the employees working at the institutional level. It is a matter of record that the employees working at Headquarters are governed by a completely different set of rules. Even the hierarchy of the posts and the channels of promotion are different Also, merely because any two posts at the Headquarters and the institutional level have the same nomenclature, would not necessarily require that the pay scales on the two posts should also be the same. The prescription of two different pay scales would not violate the principle of equal pay for equal work. Such action would not be arbitrary or violate Articles 14, 16 and 39D of the Constitution of India. It is for the employer to categorize the posts and to prescribe the duties of each post. There cannot be any straitjacket formula for holding that two posts having the same nomenclature would have to be given the same pay scale. Prescription of pay scales on particular posts is a very complex exercise. It requires assessment of the nature and quality of the duties performed and the responsibilities shouldered by the incumbents on different posts. Even though, the two posts may be referred to by the same name, it would not lead to the necessary inference that the posts are identical in every manner. These are matters to be assessed by expert bodies like the employer or the Pay Commission.

Neither the Central Administrative Tribunal nor a writ court would normally venture to substitute its own opinion for the opinions rendered by the experts. The Tribunal or the writ court would lack the necessary expertise to undertake the complex exercise of equation of posts or the pay scales.

Judgment and order dated 8.8.2008 of High Court of Punjab and Haryana at Chandigarh in C.W.P. No. 9595-CAT of 2004, affirmed.

Brief Facts:

The Appellant was initially appointed as a Laboratory Assistant in Group D on 29th December, 1961 in the National Dairy Research Institute (hereinafter referred to as 'NDRI'). On 13th January, 1966, he was promoted as a Lower Division Clerk (Junior Clerk) after qualifying limited departmental competitive examination. He was further promoted on 10th May, 1973 as a Senior Clerk, again after qualifying limited departmental competitive examination. At that stage, his pay scale was Rs. 1200-2040/-. Subsequently, on 15th June, 1988, he was promoted to the post of Superintendent in the pay scale of Rs. 1640-2900/- after passing the departmental examination. On 17th March, 1994, he was promoted as Assistant Administrative Officer on the basis of seniority-cum-fitness. The Respondent revised the pay scale of Assistants on 17th June, 1995 from Rs. 1400-2600, to Rs. 1640-2900/- w.e.f. 1st January, 1986. However, the pay scale of Superintendent was not revised.

Held, while dismissing the petition:

i. Undoubtedly, the doctrine of 'equal pay for equal work' is not an abstract doctrine and is capable of being enforced in a court of law. But equal pay must be for equal work of equal value. The principle of 'equal pay for equal work' has no mechanical application in every case. Article 14 permits reasonable classification based on qualities or characteristics of persons recruited and grouped together, as against those who were left out. of course, the qualities or characteristics must have a reasonable relation to the object sought to be achieved. In service matters, merit or experience can be a proper basis for classification for the purposes of pay in order to promote efficiency in administration. *A higher pay scale to avoid stagnation or resultant frustration for lack of promotional avenues is also an acceptable reason for pay differentiation....*

A mere nomenclature designating a person as say a carpenter or a craftsman is not enough to come to the conclusion that he is doing the same work as another carpenter or craftsman in regular service. The quality of work which is produced may be different and even the nature of work assigned may be different. It is not just a comparison of physical activity. The application of the principle of 'equal pay for equal work' requires consideration of various dimensions of a given job. The accuracy required and the dexterity that the job may entail may differ from job to job. It cannot be judged by the mere volume of work. There may be qualitative difference as regards reliability and responsibility. Functions may be the same but the responsibilities make a difference. Thus normally the applicability of this principle must be left to be evaluated and determined by an expert body. These are not matters where a writ court can lightly interfere. Normally a party claiming equal pay for equal work should be required to raise a dispute in this regard. In any event, the party who claims equal pay for equal work has to make necessary averments and prove that all things are equal. Thus, before any direction can be issued by a court, the court must first see that there are necessary averments and there is a proof.

(Emphasis supplied)

i. In our opinion, the aforesaid observations would be a complete answer to all the submissions made by the Appellant.
ii. For the aforesaid reasons, we see no merit in this appeal and the same is dismissed.

NINETEEN

STATE OF HARYANA AND ORS. VS. CHARANJIT SINGH AND ORS., 2005

Hon'ble Judges/Coram:

S.N. Variava, A.R. Lakshmanan and S.H. Kapadia, JJ.

Equivalent Citation: 2006(38)AIC151, AIR2006SC161, AIR2006SC161, 2006(1)ALT4(SC), [2005(107)FLR994], JT2005(12)SC475, 2005LabIC4322, (2006)ILLJ431SC, 2005(4)LLN949(SC), 2006(1)PLJR176, 2005(8)SCALE482, (2006)9SCC321, (2006)SCC(LS)1804, 2006(3)SCT681(SC), 2005(6)SLR693(SC), MANU/SC/1298/2005

Relevant sections: Article 14 of the Constitution of India

Number of pages in original Judgment: 11

Case Note:

Service - Equal Pay for Equal Work - Constitution of India, Article 14 - Respondents-petitioners were daily wagers, who were appointed as ledger clerks, ledger keepers, pump operators, mali-cum-chowkidar, fitters, petrol men, surveyors etc - Petitions were filed by respondents-petitioners before the High Court claiming that they should be paid minimum wages, payable under the pay-scale of regular Class IV employees from the date of their appointments - The Full Bench of High Court directed that the respondents-petitioners should be given minimum wages in the pay scale payable to regular Class IV employee from the date of filing of respective petition -

Hence, the present appeals against the judgment of the High Court - Whilst these appeals were pending before the Court, all the respondents-petitioners had been regularized - From the date of their regularization, the respondents-petitioners were paid pay scales as payable to regular Class IV employee - Appellants-respondent contended that respondents-petitioners entitled to get minimum wages only from the date of regularization - Respondents-petitioners contended that applying the principle of "equal pay for equal work", they were entitled to get the minimum pay scale from the date of their employment as casual employees or daily wagers - Held, principle of "equal pay for equal work" has no mechanical application in every case Article 14 permits reasonable classification based on qualities or characteristics of persons recruited and grouped together, as against those who were left out - High Court had blindly proceeded on the basis that the doctrine of equal pay for equal work applies without examining any relevant factors - All the impugned judgments were set aside and all the matters were remitted back to the High Court.

Brief Facts:

i. In all these Appeals, the Respondents were daily wagers who were appointed as ledger clerks, ledger keepers, pump operators, mali-cum-chowkidar, fitters, petrol men, surveyors etc. All of them claimed the minimum wages payable under the pay-scale of regular Class IV employees from the date of their appointments. The question whether or not these persons were entitled to the minimum of the pay-scale of a regular Class IV employee was referred to a Full Bench for consideration. The Full Bench gave its decision. Following the Full Bench decision all these Writ Petitions have been disposed off with short Orders. In all these cases the Respondents have been directed to be given the minimum of the wages in the scale payable to a regular Class IV employee from the date of the filing of the respective Petition.
ii. One other fact which must be mentioned is that, whilst these Appeals were pending before this Court, all the Respondents have been regularized. From the date of their regularization they being paid pay-scales as payable to a regular Class IV employee. The question therefore is only whether the directions of the High Court to pay the minimum wage in the scale payable to a Class IV employee, from the date of their filing the respective Petition, is required to be interfered with.

iii. When these Appeals came up for hearing on 23rd August, 2004 this Court referred the matters to a larger Bench for consideration by passing the following Order:

"The respondents in all these appeals were initially appointed as Ledger-clerks, ledger keepers, pump operators, mali-cum-chowkidars, fitters, petrol man, surveyor, drivers etc. on daily wages or on contractual basis. They were all regularized with effect from October, 2003 and they have been getting the minimum payable under the regular pay scale of Class-IV employees from the date of their regularization. In the writ petitions filed by these respondents before the High Court of Punjab and Haryana at Chandigarh, the Division Bench directed that these respondents shall be paid the minimum salary and dearness allowances payable to their counter parts working on regular basis. The question for consideration before this Court, in the present set of cases, is that whether these respondents are entitled to get the minimum scale of pay from the date of their appointment as daily wagers/casual employees or they are entitled to get the minimum salary in the scale of pay from the date of their regularization.

Held, while disposing off the petitions:

i. We, therefore, set aside all the impugned Judgments and remit all these matters back to the High Court. The High Court shall now examine each case and see whether the necessary averments are there. It shall then consider all relevant facts, as enumerated above, and decide whether everything is identical and equal. If the High Court feels that there is a dispute which would necessitate extensive evidence it may direct that party to raise an appropriate dispute where such questions could be dealt with and which, in fact, would be the appropriate proceedings.
ii. One other fact which must be noted is that Civil Appeals Nos. 6648 of 2002, 6647 of 2002, 6572 of 2002 and 6570 of 2002 do not deal with casual or daily rated workers. These are cases of persons employed on contract. To such persons the principles of equal pay for equal work has no application. The Full Bench Judgment dealt only with daily rated and casual workers. Where a person is employed under a contract, it is the contract which will govern the terms and conditions of service. In the case of State of Haryana v. Surinder Kumar and Ors., reported in MANU/SC/0516/1997: [1997]2SCR917, persons employed on contract basis claimed equal pay as regular workers on the footing that their

posts were interchangeable. It was held that these persons had no right to the regular posts until they are duly selected and appointed. It was held that they were not entitled to the same pay as regular employees by claiming that they are discharging same duties. It was held that the very object of selection is to test eligibility and then to make appointment in accordance with rules. It was held that the Respondents had not been recruited in accordance with the rules prescribed for recruitment.

iii. In the case of Union of India and Ors. v. K.V. Baby and Anr., reported in MANU/SC/1457/1998: (1999)ILLJ1290SC , the question was whether Commission Bearers/Vendors are entitled to the same salary as regular employees. It was held that their appointment and mode of selection, their qualifications cannot be compared with regular employees. It was held that by their very nature of employment they cannot be equated with regular employees. It was held that recruitment rules and service conditions do not apply to such persons. It was held that their responsibilities cannot be equated with those of regular employees.

iv. Thus it is clear that persons employed on contract cannot claim equal pay on basis on equal pay for equal work. Faced with this situation it was submitted that all these persons were in fact claiming that their respective appointments were regular appointments by the regular process of appointment but that instead of giving regular appointments they were appointed on contract with the intention of not paying them regular salary. It was admitted that the Petitions may be badly drafted and such a contention not put forth specifically. The High Court has disposed of these Petitions also on the footing that the principle of equal pay for equal work applied. We therefore set aside the impugned orders in these cases also and remit the matters back to the High Court for disposal. The High Court shall permit these Petitioners to amend their Petitions to make necessary averments and will also permit the Respondents in these cases to file replies to the amended Petitions.

v. With the above directions all these Appeals stand disposed off. All the matters are remitted back to the High Court. There will be no order as to costs.

TWENTY

M.P. Rural Agriculture Extension Officers Association Vs. State of M.P. and Ors., 2004

Hon'ble Judges/Coram:

V.N. Khare, C.J., S.B. Sinha and S.H. Kapadia, JJ.

Equivalent Citation: 2004(19)AIC836, AIR2004SC2020, 2004(4)ALT15(SC), [2004(101)FLR691], [2004(3)JCR16(SC)], 2005(1)JLJ36(SC), JT2004(4)SC446, 2004(2)KLT265(SC), 2004LabIC1727, (2004)IILLJ1114SC, 2004(2)LLN729(SC), (2004)3MLJ139(SC), 2004(4)SCALE260, (2004)4SCC646, 2004(2)SCT431(SC), 2005(1)SLJ12(SC), 2004(3)SLR305(SC), 2004(2)UJ1283, MANU/SC/0546/2004

Relevant sections: Article 14 and 39(d) of the Constitution of India

Number of pages in original Judgment: 07

Case Note:

Constitution of India - Articles 14 and 39 (d)--Employment--Doctrine of 'equal pay for equal work'--Extension officers--Pay Commission recommending same scale of pay to be given irrespective of their educational qualification--But State Government differenting graduate officers and non-graduate officers in respect of pay scale--Whether justified? -- Held, "yes"-- Classification based on educational qualification is valid.

Brief Facts:

i. The appellant herein is an Association of Rural Agriculture Extension Officers (hereinafter referred to as 'the Extension Officers'). They were originally appointed as Village Level Workers. They are matriculates. The services of the Village Level Workers were transferred to the agriculture department of the State. It framed rules in the year 1972. On or about 9.4.1981, the designation of the Village Level Workers was changed to the Rural Agriculture Extension Officer by the State Government. The State of Madhya Pradesh in exercise of the power conferred upon it under the Proviso appended to Article 309 of the Constitution of India made rules known as 'Madhya Pradesh Revision of Pay Rules, 1983'. Rule 3 of the said rules reads as under:--

"Revised Scale of Pay.--The revised scale of pay applicable to any post carrying existing scale shown in columns 2 and 3 of Annexures I and II respectively shall be the corresponding pay scale shown in column 4 thereof respect of that post."

i. By reason of the provisions of the said Rules, two different scales of pay were prescribed, namely, Rs. 575-880/- for non-graduates (Dying scale) and Rs. 635-950/-for fresh recruitment and for existing B.Sc./ 13.Sc. Agriculture. By reason of an executive instruction dated 2/5.3.1984, the decision of the State Government was communicated to the Director, Agriculture, the relevant portion whereof is to the following effect :--

"Essential educational qualification for the post of Rural Agricultural Extension Officer being graduation (for all departments) be fixed and all the graduates so employed be paid by the pay-scale of Rs. 635/950. All those graduate employees who were working to the posts in all departments prior to 1.4.1981 should be paid given a salary at the rate of Rs. 635-950/-.

Held, while dismissing the petition:

True it may be that when recommendations are made by a Pay Commission, evaluation of job must be held to have been made but the same by itself may not be a ground to enforce the recommendations by issuing a writ of or in the nature of mandamus although the State did not accept the same in toto and made rules to the contrary by evolving a policy decision which cannot be said to arbitrary or discriminatory.

For the reasons aforementioned, we are of the opinion that no case has been made for our interference with the impugned judgment. The appeal is dismissed accordingly. No costs.

Videos & Tv Shows On Law & Exim

List of some important videos & TV shows on Law & EXIM by Adv. Jayprakash Somani on his YouTube Channel 'Jayprakash Somani EXIM & Legal'

Legal Videos: Hindi -English

1) SLP in Supreme Court / Special Leave Petitions in the Supreme Court of India

2) Transfer of Civil & Criminal Cases by the Supreme Court of India / Transfer of Matrimonial Cases

3) Appellate Jurisdiction of the Supreme Court of India

4) Jurisdictions of the Supreme Court of India

5) Public Interest Litigation in the Supreme Court of India / PIL in Supreme Court

6) Article 32 Writ Petitions in the Supreme Court of India

7) Bail Matters Top 10 Supreme Court Cases

8) FIR Quashing in High Court & Supreme Court

9) Bail & Anticipatory Bail Matters in Supreme Court

10) Insolvency & Bankruptcy Matters in the Supreme Court

11) Insolvency & Bankruptcy Code 2016 Part 1

12) Insolvency & Bankruptcy Code 2016 Part 2

13) Insolvency & Bankruptcy Code 2016 Part 3

14) Corporate Liquidation Process

15) Supreme Court Rules & Procedures Webinar of 2.5 hour on Zoom

16) RDDBFI Act, 1993 (Introduction)

17) The Indian Contact Act 1872

18) Negotiable Instruments Act (Introduction)

19) How to avoid matrimonial disputes& some more videos

20)SEBI Matters in the Supreme Court

21) Matrimonial Matters: Supreme Court's 20 Case Laws

22) Consumer Matters Supreme Court's 20 Case Laws

23) Service Matters Supreme Court's 20 Case Laws

24) How to Search Lawyer for Your Matter

25) Property Matters Supreme Court's 20 Case Laws

26) Bail Matters: Supreme Court's 20 Case Laws

27) Supreme Court / High Court Vacation Benches

28)69000 Teacher's Recruitment Matters of UP Government in the Supreme Court

29) Contempt of Court Matters in the Supreme Court

30) Advocate Act's Matters in the Supreme Court

31) Business Law Matters in the Supreme Court

32) Banking Matters in the Supreme Court

33) Labour Law Matters in the Supreme Court

34) Arbitration Matters in the Supreme Court

35) Careers in Law -Zoom Webinar by Adv. Jayprakash Somani

36) Civil Matters in the Supreme Court

37) Consumer Protection Act | Consumer Matters in the Supreme Court

38) Corporate Matters in the Supreme Court

39) Criminal Matters in the Supreme Court

40) Role of Respondent in the Supreme Court of India

41) Motor Vehicle Accident Matters in Supreme Court with case laws

42) Article 131 Original Suits in Supreme Court

43)PIL in Supreme Court/ Public Interest Litigations in the Supreme Court of India'

44)CAB Citizenship Amendment Bill is not Unconstitutional

45) Supreme Court of India Cases & Process – Marathi

46) Legal Services Export / Export of Legal Services

47) Transfer of Matrimonial Cases by the Supreme Court of India

48) Public Interest Litigation PIL

49) The Specific Relief Act (Introduction)

50) Corporate Insolvency Resolution Process CIRP

51)ABMM's Career 5 - Careers in Law

52) Transfer of cases by Supreme Court

53) Writ Petitions in High Court & Supreme Court of India

54) Supreme Court Jurisdictions - Appeals, SLP, Writ Petitions, Transfer, Original, Review, Curative

55)LEGAL INDIA TV Show: Cases Handled in Supreme Court

56) Corporate Liquidation Process

57) Legal Services Export / Export of Legal Services

EXIM Videos: Hindi -English

1) Yes, I can do Import Export Business Easily! 36 points excellent video in Hindi

2) Yes, I can do Import Export Business Easily! 36 points excellent video in English

3) Import Export Business – Hindi video

4) Import Export Business - English video

5) Export Import Marathi TV Interview

6) Scope for Commerce Students in International Business- TV Show

7) Scope for Management Student in International Business- TV Show

8) Scope for Engineering Students in International Business – TV Show

9) Women in International Business- TV Show

10) How to do Import Export Business Successfully!'

11) Where one can get full information on Import Export Business?

12) What to do import & export?

13) Import Export Workshop/ Training/Course/ Diploma

14) How to Start Import Export Business & How to grow it. Live Webinar

15) Success Stories & Failure Stories in Import & Export Business

16) For MSME Scope in Export & Import...

17) Exports In Agri. & Food Products – English & some more videos

18) Exports to Dubai, Aabudhabii. e. UAE

19) Jewelry Exports from India

20) Ilow to attend EXIM workshop to bccomc cxccllcnt Exporter

21) Import Export Best Training Course – Online & Offline

22) Agri Product Export

23) Scope for Woman in International Business

24) Management Graduates Scope in International Business

25) Pharma Product's Export

26) Best Import Export Course | Practical Training | Aaronica Global Exim

27) Import Export Business for Commerce Graduates

28) How Do I Get Export Orders? Finding International Buyers

29) What Is APEDA In Import Export Business?

30) Which Is The Best Product To Export From India?

31)EXIM Remark by Manoj Kumar Faridabad

32)EXIM Remarks by Mahesh Telangana

33) What Licenses I Need To Start Import/ Export?

34) How Can I Increase My Import Export Business?

35) Which Is Best B2B Website For Import/Export Business?

36) Export Import Management with Global Marketing

37) How to Start Export Import Business | 51 Points Video

38) Scope for Commerce & Other Graduates in International Business
39)BE A SUCCESSFUL EXPORTER FOR OUR NATION - Marathi video
40) Export of Textile , Cotton, Agri., Food, & other products & services
41) Exports from MP, CG, MH, GJ & CA in Fresh Fruits & Vegetables
42) Exports in Agri. & Food Products- Hindi
43) Start your Online/E-Commerce Business
44) How to Start Export Import Business & Grow it
45) Exports in Textile & Other Products
46) Start and grow EXIM business - Live English Webinar
47)'Import Export Business!' Why, Who, What &How can one do it easily!!
48) Live: Export of Product & Services During & After Lock Down Period
49) Frauds in Import Export Business
50) Import Export for Business Man
51) Import& Export for Women
51) Import& Export for Graduate & Post - Graduate Students
52) Agriculture Exports from India
53) Digital Marketing Setup - Marathi
54)2nd Secret of Successful Businessman
55) Digital Marketing Set up
56) Legal Services Export / Export of Legal Services
57) Export& Import with UAE
58) Service Exports / Exports by Service Providers
59) Import Export Workshop/ Training/Course/ Diploma
60) Exports& Imports with USA
61) Selection on Product for Export
62) Top Products Exported from India
63) What to do import & export?
64)ABMM Career 2 - 'Careers in Business & Industries
65) How to do Import Export Business Successfully!'
66)5 Secrets of Successful Businessman
67) Export from MP, Chhattisgarh &Vidarbha Nagpur
68)EXIM Hindi - Textile & Apparel Export
69)EXIM Hindi - Export Import Practical Training In Delhi, Kolkata, Mumbai and Pune
70) Import Export Business
71) Import Export Business Hindi
72) Import Export Business English video

73) Import Export Business Marathi

74) Women in International Business by Exim Guru Adv. Jayprakash Somani

75) Opportunities in Foreign Trade- Adv. Jayprakash Somani's special interview

List Of Adv. Jayprakash Somani's Books

1. Supreme Court of India's Leading Case Laws on 'Insolvency & Bankruptcy Code 2016'

2. Bail Matters – Supreme Court's Latest Leading Case Laws

3. Arbitration Matters- Supreme Court's Latest Leading Case Laws

4. Property Matters - Supreme Court's Latest Leading Case Laws

5. Matrimonial Matters- Supreme Court's Latest Leading Case Laws

6. Election Matters- Supreme Court's Latest Leading Case Laws

7.SEBI Matters- Supreme Court's Latest Leading Case Laws

8. Banking Matters- Supreme Court's Latest Leading Case Laws

9. Service Matters- Supreme Court's Latest Leading Case Laws

10. Contempt of Court Matters- Supreme Court's Latest Leading Case Laws

11. Consumer Protection Matters- Supreme Court's Latest Leading Case Laws

12. Corporate Law- Supreme Court's Latest Leading Case Laws

13. Supreme Court's AOR Exam- Leading Cases

14. Armed Force Tribunal - Supreme Court's Latest Leading Case Laws

15. Acquittal From 376 - Supreme Court's Latest Leading Case Laws

16. Negotiable instrument – Supreme Court's Latest Leading Case Laws

17. Contract Act- Supreme Court's Latest Leading Case Laws

18. Insider trading- Supreme Court's Latest Leading Case Laws

19. Foreign Exchange and Management Act- Supreme Court's Latest Leading Case Laws

20. Income Tax Act- Supreme Court's Latest Leading Case Laws

21. Company Law- Supreme Court's Latest Leading Case Laws

22. Competition & Monopoly Matters- Supreme Court's Latest Leading Case Laws

23. Compassionate Appointment- Service Matters- Supreme Court's Latest Leading Case Laws

24. Compulsory Retirement- Service Matters- Supreme Court's Latest Leading Case Laws

25. Voluntary Retirement- Service Matters- Supreme Court's Latest Leading Case Laws

26. Removal/Dismissal/Termination from Service- Supreme Court's Latest Leading Case Laws

27. Seniority- Service Matter- Supreme Court's Latest Leading Case Laws

28. Promotion- Service Matter- Supreme Court's Latest Leading Case Laws

29. Equal Pay for Equal Work- Service Matter- Supreme Court's Latest Leading Case Laws

ÞÞÞ

These Books are available online at

1. **Notion Press:** https://notionpress.com/author/jayprakash_somani
2. **Amazon:** https://www.amazon.in/s?k=jayprakash+somani
3. **Flipkart:** https://www.flipkart.com/search?q=Jayprakash%20Somani

ÞÞÞ

9 798885 693448

Printed by Libri Plureos GmbH in Hamburg, Germany